The
Tao of
Womanhood

女

WILLIAM MORROW
AND COMPANY, INC.

New York

# The Tao of Womanhood

## TEN LESSONS
## FOR POWER
## AND PEACE

Diane Dreher

26074377

299.51444082

DRE

Library of Congress Cataloging-in-Publication Data

Dreher, Diane, 1946–
      The Tao of womanhood : ten lessons for power and peace / Diane Dreher.
          p. cm.
      Includes bibliographical references.
      ISBN 0-688-15114-0
      1. Women—Conduct of life. 2. Lao-tzu. Tao te ching. I. Title.
BJ1610.D74 1998
299'.51444'082—dc21

                                                97-36907
                                                CIP


Printed in the United States of America

First Edition

1   2   3   4   5   6   7   8   9   10

BOOK DESIGN BY DEBORAH KERNER

www.williammorrow.com

*To my mother,*
*Mary Ann Hearte Dreher,*
*whose agency, courage, and grace*
*have given me a powerful model*
*of what it means to be a woman*

# Acknowledgments

I am grateful to many women whose lives have demonstrated the rich tapestry of possibilities for women today, beginning with my mother, Mary Ann Dreher, and including all the others whose stories appear in this book.

I would like to thank my agent, Sandy Dijkstra, for her enduring wisdom and belief in this project as well as Rita Holm, Sandra Zane, Julie Bennett, and Steve Malk of the Dijkstra Literary Agency for their ongoing support and encouragement. I'd like to thank my editor, Doris Cooper, for her personal commitment, editorial artistry, and shared vision as well as Joan Amico and Fritz Metsch for all they did to help the book appear in final form.

I am grateful to my *aikido sensei*, Sunny Skys, who contributed the beautiful calligraphy for this book, and to Miki Yoneda-Skys, Sue Ann McKean, and Kristie Stovall, who have shown me the power and grace of women in aikido. I would like to thank the members of the Santa Clara Writers' Group for their advice on early drafts and my women friends and colleagues in the English department at Santa Clara University, as well as Tina Clare, Sunny Merik, Carol Daeley, Mary Hegland, Maryellen Mori, Katherine Woodall, and

Elizabeth Moran for their valuable advice along the way. A final vote of thanks goes to my husband, Robert Numan, for his combination of wisdom, love, and humor that helps make my life a journey of joy and discovery.

The *Tao Te Ching* gives us a vision of life as a dynamic, evolving pattern in which nothing exists in isolation. Accordingly, a portion of the royalties from this book will be donated to support services for women at risk, ongoing work in conflict resolution, and other projects that help create a more powerful and peaceful future for us all.

# Contents

# *Illustrations*

*Frontispiece. Woman:* Chinese *nū*, Japanese *onna*, the character for woman. Originally, the character depicted woman bowing or kneeling to others. I like to see it as bowing to the greater potential within ourselves.

*Introduction: Power and Peace. Power:* Chinese *lì*, Japanese *chikara*. This character for "strength" is derived from a pictograph of an arm with a strong biceps. Here it stands for a woman's own sense of agency or personal power. The character is repeated in the Pointers for Power and Peace that conclude each chapter and the Glossary at the end of the book. *Peace:* Chinese *ān*, Japanese *an shin*. This character represents a woman sitting peacefully under her own roof.

*Part I: The Yin of Inner Peace.* Chinese *yin*, Japanese *in*. One of the twin polarities that comprise all existence, the character originally meant the shady side of a hill. *Yin* is shadow, contemplative, nurturing, inner. In this book, the *yin* section focuses on lessons of inner peace, while the *yang* section focuses on personal power. Yet both are as inseparable as breathing in and breathing out, together manifesting our full potential as women.

*Chapter 1: The Lesson of Oneness. Nature: Shizen* in Japanese is a complex character that means "the way things should be," made up of the character *shi* for "self" combined with *zen*, "contentment." Chapter 1 balances an awareness of the patterns around us with care of the self to create "the way things should be" in our lives.

*Chapter 2: The Lesson of Centering. Center:* The Chinese character *zhōng*, meaning "middle" or "center." Chapter 2 reminds us to center in on what is most important in order to maintain our inner balance.

*Chapter 3: The Lesson of Compassion. Compassion:* This character combines the Japanese characters for "gate" or "house," *mon;* "person," *jin;* and "heart-mind," *shin.* Chapter 3 shows how to open the gates of our hearts.

*Chapter 4: The Lesson of Simplicity. Misogi,* the Japanese character for ritualistic purification, is made up of the characters for "shrine" and "sacred pledge." Chapter 4 encourages us to simplify our lives, clearing away clutter to create more space for contemplation and peace of mind.

*Chapter 5: The Lesson of Natural Cycles. Shiki,* the Japanese character for "seasons," is made up of the number four and the character for young rice plants growing in the spring. Chapter 5 shows how our lives repeat on many levels the four seasons of spring, summer, fall, and winter.

*Part II: The Yang of Personal Power.* Chinese *yang,* Japanese *yō.* One of the twin polarities that comprise all existence, the character originally meant the sunny side of a hill. *Yang* is sunshine, action, outward expression. In this book, the *yang* section focuses on personal power, while the *yin* section promotes inner peace. Yet both are as inseparable as mountains and valleys, together manifesting our full potential as women.

*Chapter 6: The Lesson of Timing. Musubi:* The Japanese character is made up of the two characters for "thread" and "good luck," to mean a fortunate joining together of circumstances. In Chapter 6, we learn how to practice effective timing in our lives, remaining centered while blending our energies with other people and events.

*Chapter 7: The Lesson of Courage. Hara:* The Japanese character means literally the body's center or "belly." To have *hara* means to act with heart, courage, or resolve. Chapter 7 shows how to face our fears and move forward in life with courage.

*Chapter 8: The Lesson of Strength. Water:* Chinese *shui,* Japanese *mizu.* Water is an archetypal image of Tao. Gentle, nurturing, the source of all life, it is strong enough to cut through solid rock. Drawing upon these qualities, Chapter 8 gives us a new definition of strength that combines the polarities of power and peace.

*Chapter 9: The Lesson of Agency. Mindfulness:* This character combines the Japanese characters *ryū,* "to connect or fasten," and *shin,* "heart-mind." Chapter 9 shows us how we can become active agents by overcoming old feelings of powerlessness and meeting life's challenges more mindfully.

*Chapter 10: The Lesson of Harmony. Bamboo:* Chinese *zhú,* Japanese *chiku.* Bamboo is a symbol of fortitude and endurance in Asian art. Chapter 10 shows us how to use the strength of bamboo to transform challenge and conflict into harmony.

*Glossary. Power:* Chinese *li,* Japanese *chikara,* the character for "strength," which also occurs in the Pointers for Power and Peace that end each chapter.

*Notes. Tao:* Chinese *tao,* Japanese *dō,* the first character in the *Tao Te Ching* and the final character in the book, *tao* is the way, the ongoing journey of our lives.

# Introduction

Hold to your heart
The wisdom of Tao
Because through it
We discover
Our own answers,
Learn the ways
Of power and peace,
And find the greatest treasure
Under heaven.

*T A O ,  6 2* [1]

One of my favorite treasures from childhood is a black-lacquered jewelry box my father gave me when I was ten. Brought back from one of his many flights to Tokyo when we lived in the Philippines, it was the most beautiful gift I'd ever seen. On the top, framed by iridescent mother-of-pearl, is a painted journey through groves of bamboo and cherry blossoms, past a shining pagoda, over a curved bridge to a house on a golden island. Inside is a lining of rose brocade, a double mirror, and a music box that plays "China Night." Worn by time and filled with memories, the small lacquered box rests on a table in my study, its painted story still bright after all these years.

In my living room is a new treasure, yet older still, a Chinese wedding chest from the 1860s, about eighteen inches long, covered with hand-tooled leather and layers of red lacquer. Decorated with gold-leaf characters for harmony and double happiness, it was a wedding gift from my women friends at Santa Clara University where I teach.

Originally used for letters and wedding invitations, the red-lacquered box is richly symbolic. The "double happiness" characters are traditional good wishes for a married couple. Yet, since this was a gift from my women friends, the twin characters also represent for me the dual aspects of a woman's life, the public and private, inside and outside, *yin* and *yang* of her existence, the stories she shares with others and those she keeps in her heart.

Between these two treasured gifts in my life, the jewelry box from my girlhood and the wedding box of adulthood, there are many stories. Some of them are in this book.

WOMEN HAVE always told each other stories. Around the old kitchens, my grandmother and her twin sister would spend hours telling stories as they made pies, biscuits, dumplings, and other specialties from their home in south Texas. I remember sitting in their kitchens, surrounded by the fragrance of cinnamon and apples, listening to stories of past and present that took me back many lifetimes, into a world of dreams.

Throughout women's history, in kitchens, over sewing and knitting, from quilting bees to consciousness-raising groups to intimate conversations with our best friends, women have always told each other stories. Weaving together experiences and insights, analyzing the important relationships and challenges in our lives, this is how we discover our wisdom.

There are so many stories, so many ways to be a woman today. From the Renaissance to the early twentieth century, handbooks for women—usually written by men—upheld a static feminine ideal. Today, there can be no single definition of womanhood. There is, rather, an ongoing journey of discovery, a "way," as in the Tao of ancient China, with nature's dynamic patterns evolving into personal manifestations uniquely our own.

This book is filled with stories, views of many women's lives. Some women are famous; some are my friends and neighbors. Some you will recognize; others you will never meet. Like the jewelry box from my childhood, this book portrays life's journey, containing its own double mirror of past and present, self and others, reflections of many women's lives. As you trace the patterns in these pages, you'll find yourself in some of them. In others, contrasting colors will give you new perspectives on your life.

Rich with the traditions of the past, filled with the promise of a future that only you can create, this book blends women's stories with lessons of power and peace from the ancient Chinese classic, the *Tao Te Ching*. It offers a path to greater wholeness and balance, dispelling the half-truths we've inherited. For women today, gaining power does not mean sacrificing our peace of mind, and living in peace does not mean subordinating ourselves to others and losing our personal power. The wisdom of Tao reveals how we can experience greater power and peace by embracing life more mindfully, becoming more fully ourselves.

As you hold this book in your hands, it is like my red-lacquered box, touching the lives of many women, past and present, open to new possibilities for your life today. Sit down with the book as you would with a friend. Read, reflect, and tell yourself your own story, adding your own double happiness to the blend of centuries and discovering for yourself the Tao of Womanhood.

Offering an empowering path for all women, the wisdom of Tao influences not so much what you do but how you do it. Whether you live alone, with a partner, or in the family pattern as a wife and mother, whether your life's work lies inside or outside the home, following the Tao will help you become more creative, proactive, and optimistic. Instead of being a victim of circumstance, dominated and driven by externals, you'll draw strength from enduring principles. Moving assuredly, you'll take greater charge of your life and act from center, from your own deepest sense of yourself. You'll learn the Taoist lesson of timing: when to act, when to pause and reflect, when to seize an opportunity, when to spend time with a child or troubled friend, when to take that necessary time for yourself.

Following the Tao means becoming more aware of life's patterns, being open and flexible, embracing new opportunities for learning and growth. It means gracefully blending with life's changes, knowing that moving forward need not be frantic or reactive. Even if you're momentarily thrown off balance, you'll know how to return to center and learn from the process.

FOR OVER two thousand years, artists and innovators in many fields have been inspired by the *Tao Te Ching*. Translated more often than any book but the Bible, this ancient Chinese classic of eighty-one lyric poems has endured because its message of harmony and dynamic growth is as real today as it was twenty-five centuries ago.

The *Tao Te Ching* was written by the philosopher Lao-tzu during the warring-states period in ancient China, about 530 B.C. Seeking alternatives to conflict and chaos, Lao-tzu found inspiration walking in the woods, observing the lessons in a mountain stream, a grove of bamboo, and the changing seasons. By studying nature's principles, he found in Taoism an enduring philosophy of power and peace, a way to transform life's challenges into opportunities for personal renewal.

*Tao* means "the path" or "the way of life." In *The Tao of Womanhood* it becomes a new way of seeing life, a way of living more mindfully, combining the polarities of power and peace. Becoming more aware of your own life's journey and the recurrent cycles of nature will help you recognize the energy patterns within and around you. You'll gain a new definition of strength that combines forcefulness and flexibility, nurturing and assertiveness, action and contemplation, powerful principles that can bring greater joy and meaning to your life.

Both practical and inspirational, the *Tao*'s message of power and peace holds vital lessons for us today. Our complex world presents us with a vast array of challenges and choices, along with conflicting definitions, demands, and expectations about what it means to be a woman.

The tempo of life in our highly industrialized society is geared to mechanical efficiency and bottom-line economics. Pulling us away from our own natural wisdom, it often leaves us feeling frantic, exhausted, and disconnected. The way of Tao asks us to withdraw from the noise and confusion, the push and pull of external demands, long enough to listen to ourselves, to consider what is most important, to touch the intuitive wisdom deep in our hearts. As we take this opportunity to live more mindfully, we can move from frantic reaction to focused action.

The gentle way of Tao returns us to the wisdom of nature, helping us to uncover the depths of our own nature in the process. Simply and eloquently, the Tao reminds us of nature's patterns. The ebb and flow of the tides, the phases of the moon, the changing seasons of our lives—all are variations on the cycles that occur not only in the natural world but also in individuals, families, and relationships. Whatever your current age or stage in life, the principles of Tao can help you make wiser choices by recognizing these patterns.

## DISCOVERING YOUR OWN NATURE

WOMEN'S LIVES today are filled with paradox. We are expected to be beautiful, required to be strong, like a fine piece of Chinese embroidery with its shining silk threads sewn into intricate and demanding patterns. Asked to do so many things, we are often torn between polarities, caught up in the active life, yet longing for more of the contemplative. Do you want to be more powerful, more confident, more authentically yourself while finding greater peace of mind? The lessons in this book will help you find your own answers, combining life's varied strands into your own personal tapestry of power and peace.

Living on the edge of the twenty-first century, we are more than our mothers' daughters. The old images of womanhood fit us as poorly as hand-me-down clothing. But the newly tailored expectations are often equally uncomfortable. As long as we seek to live by external standards, we can never quite measure up. For as the *Tao* reminds us, we can find fulfillment only by being true to our own nature.

Personal empowerment is evident in the title of the *Tao Te Ching* itself. *Ching* means a sacred book; *Tao*, the journey of our lives; while *Te* means our essential nature. It is made up of three characters: "to go," "straight," and "the heart." Thus, the Tao is a journey of discovery and fulfillment that leads straight from the heart.

Drawing upon the *Tao*'s vital lessons, this book will help you develop your own definition of what it means to be a woman. Instead of offering another list of "shoulds," which women have in excess, the way of Tao emphasizes wholeness and integrity. It reminds us that we are more than the roles we play: more than mother, daughter, sister, student, girlfriend, wife, career woman, or grandmother. Such roles are static and reductive. Like the palette of an Impressionist painter, any woman's life is a subtle blending of many colors, many gradations of sunlight and shadow, as naturally varied as the patterns in a living landscape. The insights and spiritual exercises in this book will help you develop greater vision, courage, and resourcefulness, creating a style of womanhood uniquely your own.[2]

## THE WISDOM OF *YIN* AND *YANG*

TRADITIONALLY, WOMEN have shaped their lives around relationships and interdependence while men have valued power and abstract principles.[3] Over the centuries, women's concern with relationships has been both a chronic weakness and an enduring strength, contributing to the care and nurturing of generations, while depriving women as individuals. When taken to extremes, our concern with relationships produces overly compliant women who never think for themselves. While caring for others is essential to life, an attitude of perpetual self-sacrifice can become pathological and self-destructive.[4]

As the currents of life today pull women between opposing impulses of nurturing and assertiveness, we can find harmony in the dynamic message of the *Tao*, which portrays all of nature—including human nature—as composed of both the compassionate, nurturing energies of *yin* and the forceful, assertive energies of *yang*. Following the *Tao* keeps us from falling into the false dilemma of choosing either *yin* or *yang*, reminding us that a complete life must include both. Instead of exhausting our energies by conforming to limited stereotypes or singlemindedly rebelling against them, trying too hard to be either "feminine" or "strong," we can transcend domination by *either* extreme. The *Tao*'s vision of wholeness includes polarities in dynamic balance—public and private, active and contemplative. In a balanced life, these opposites alternate as naturally as breathing in and breathing out.

The stories and personal exercises in this book will help you develop a deeper understanding of the two mighty opposites of *yin* and *yang* in your life. You'll learn when a single extreme becomes unhealthy, even dangerous. Too much passivity or compliance produces an imbalance within yourself and your relationships that ripples outward, leading to greater imbalance in the world around you. To avoid such an imbalance, you'll learn how to nurture yourself as well as others, combining *yin* and *yang* to bring greater harmony to your life and your world.

You'll also learn a new definition of strength. The imagery in the *Tao Te Ching* upholds the strength of gentleness, the power of water, which not only nurtures life but, when focused over time, can cut through solid rock. The *Tao* also upholds the power of flexibility, the strength of bamboo, which bends but does not break. By following the lessons in this book, you'll learn to combine focus with flexibility, becoming stronger in mind and body.

## DISCOVERING THE PATTERNS OF NATURE

LIKE THE lightning flash of a Zen koan, the evocative verses of the *Tao* open up our hearts and minds, liberating us from the limits of linear thinking to reveal nature's enduring patterns and the essential wisdom deep within us. This book will help you recognize how powerfully the cycles of nature echo throughout your life.

The larger cycles are our life stages: the springtime of youth, the summer of accomplishment, the autumn of fruition, and the winter of late adulthood. As the seasons of our lives change, so do our priorities. The activities we pursued so passionately in one season may no longer make sense in another. In our twenties and thirties, many of us are busy establishing our careers, furnishing our homes, and acquiring possessions with a fervor that culminates in middle life, when we seek a new level of balance. In our later years, we often choose to simplify, scaling back, giving things away.

Within these larger cycles are smaller ones, lasting a number of years, months, or weeks. Each new job or project has its own springtime of new beginnings, summer of fulfillment, and autumn of fruition. And each cycle has its own season of winter or contemplation. When our children leave home, when we move, change careers, or face another major life transition, we pause to take stock. For everyone, there are times to reach in and times to reach out, times of *yin* and times of *yang*. This book will help you recognize the cycles in your life, finding power and joy in every season.

## 𝒯HE PLAN OF THE BOOK

TAKING YOU on an active journey of discovery, *The Tao of Womanhood* will help you chart your own path to greater power and peace. Its ten chapters are divided into two sections. "The Yin of Inner Peace" will bring you greater balance and peace of mind, while "The Yang of Personal Power" will help you develop greater focus, energy, and effectiveness. The five lessons of *yin* are followed by five lessons of *yang*, ten stepping-stones on a path to more mindful living. Each chapter leads naturally to the next, in a process of reflection, empowerment, and renewal.

Yet, like the cycles of nature, the way of Tao is more than a linear path. With insights recurrent as each day's progression of sunlight and shadow, its lessons are both unique and universal, fresh and deeply familiar. After a first reading introduces you to the way of Tao and deepens your self-awareness, you may use this book as a reference or guide to meditation, taking a section to reflect upon each day. When new challenges call you to exercise your skills in centering or timing, or old lessons recur on new levels, you can reflect upon the passages that speak to you at the time. Exercising creative choice, you can rearrange the initial stepping-stones into a new design that fits the unique and varied pattern of your life.

The ten chapters are divided into short sections, each designed to be read at a single sitting. Each chapter concludes with prescriptive exercises and pointers for greater power and peace. A Glossary at the end of the book defines important concepts, often referring you to chapters where they are explored at length. Like bright stones in a mosaic, poetic passages from the *Tao Te Ching* are scattered throughout, providing moments of beauty and inspiration to carry you through your days.

The path of *Tao* is an ongoing process of illumination and empowerment. Each day will bring you greater mindfulness, increasing your awareness of the larger patterns in your life. Reflecting upon the stories of women's lives and the recurrent principles of nature, recognizing the energies within and around you, you'll move with greater wisdom and grace. Making wiser choices and becoming more fully yourself, you'll discover new possibilities for power and peace.

I wish you joy on the path.

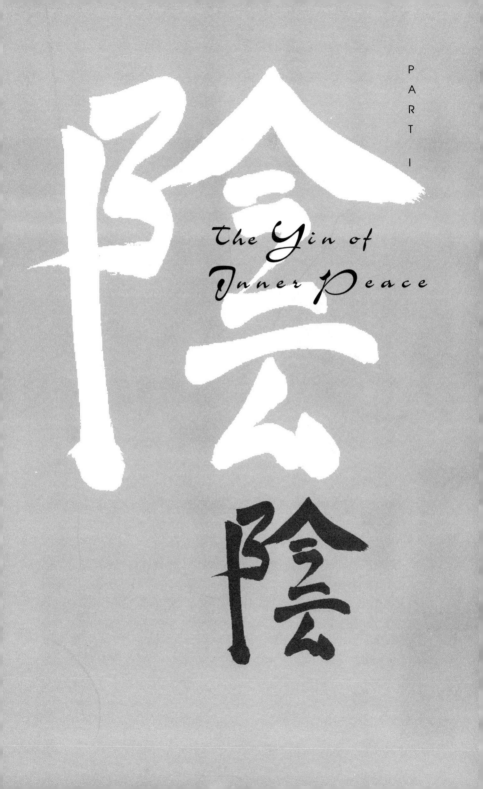

## PART I

The Yin of
Inner Peace

# The Lesson of Oneness

In the beginning was the Tao
Which gave rise to *yin* and
*yang*,
Sunlight and shadow,
And the energy
Of all existence.
Yet beneath the dance of life,
The Tao is always One,
Mother of ten thousand things,
Source of all creation.

*T A O ,   4 2*

The oneness of Tao recalls for me the winter mornings when I was eleven and awakened to a world of new-fallen snow. There, outside the window of my new home in Grandview, Missouri, was one expansive world of white— snow covering the trees and rooftops, smoothing the rough edges, blending everything into monochromatic harmony.

For children in the Midwest, snowstorms create spontaneous holidays. Roads are impassable, schools are closed, and days are dedicated to play. Eagerly downing our oatmeal and hot chocolate, donning our jackets and mittens, my brother and I would rush out into the sparkling world.

We'd crunch through the snow and ice in our boots, ride our sleds, and build snowmen. I'd watch the snowflakes as they settled on my sleeve, each one a tiny star-shaped, six-pointed crystal. A marvel of oneness in multiplicity, each snowflake was uniquely itself, while reflecting the same universal design.

Last December, my husband and I took a vacation in the High Sierra. After a busy season at work, I looked forward to cross-country skiing through silent snow-covered woods that recalled the winter playgrounds of my childhood. For a few days, at least, our hectic lives would be transformed into a winter world of white. But when we arrived, the snow was patchy except on the highest peaks.

Yet the oneness was still there. Leaving behind the crowds at Squaw Valley and Incline Village, we packed a lunch and went for a hike by the Truckee River. Its usual gentle flow was now a torrent of rushing rapids. Walking beside the powerful river through puddles and patches of snow, I found the same serenity I had when cross-country skiing or watching snowflakes as a child. Looking from the snowcapped mountains to the stream of snowmelt rushing down to the river, I saw that all these varied forms were water, the source of all life, transforming itself as it transformed the terrain. Beneath the apparent multiplicity was an underlying oneness.

Like the water whose essence endures throughout its changing forms, the oneness in your life is always there, if you know where to find it. Beneath the dance of ten thousand things on the surface, life has its own dynamic unity. The energies of *yin* and *yang*, snow and water, sunlight and shadow, alternate in our lives as well as in nature. What we are and what we do is an integral part of all that is.

Too often, as we rush from one task to the next with a chorus of voices clamoring for our attention, we see only the frantic surface of life. Yet we can regain that sense of oneness described for centuries in the Far East, carved on precious jade, painted on silk tapestries. Held within our hearts in moments of stillness, it is the essence of all Taoist art and the first lesson in the Tao of Womanhood.

## *D*YNAMIC BALANCE: FINDING UNITY IN MULTIPLICITY

RECOVERING YOUR sense of oneness, living in greater harmony, begins with a shift in perception. Conditioned by individualism and specialization, our Western minds focus on separate parts, while the wisdom of the East emphasizes relationships. Living in a world of machines, we seek a static and uniform status quo while in the world of nature life occurs in dynamic flow.

The first step in the Tao of Womanhood is realizing that you are part of the natural world, where all life is interrelated and nothing in the universe stands still. Shifting from a static to a dynamic paradigm opens your eyes to new options. As you see the relationship *among* the separate parts of your life, you'll experience more of the underlying unity.

If anyone's life is fragmented, you'd think it would be Libby's. She's a trained actress who teaches five courses a year, directs plays for her university theater, and works as an adviser in the deans' office. Married to an art professor, she has five children, two boys and three girls, ranging from seven months to fifteen years.[1]

Yet far from being frazzled and fragmented, Libby is one of the most upbeat, balanced women I know. She embraces the many facets of her life with a spirit of resilient optimism. How does she do this? Flow.

Libby met me in her theater office one May afternoon. Slim, smiling, and constantly in motion, she looks relaxed and youthful, almost like one of her students. "People ask me if I feel fragmented,"she said. "I don't. Perhaps it's because as an actress I'm used to playing many roles, perhaps it's because I've been doing this for years." Libby's dynamic view of life transforms potential fragmentation into flow. Everything is somehow part of a larger whole.

One reason she's found so much wholeness is because she sees beyond the surface, asking questions and seeking new possibilities. This year, when she began working in the deans' office, she told them she needed to find a way to continue nursing her infant son, James. "All three deans were very supportive of this," she said. But she wouldn't have had their support if she hadn't asked for it, expanding what *was* into what might be.

Her training as an actress helps Libby recognize strategic moments and manage the unexpected. "One day," she told me, "my daughter wanted to bake a cake." This was not Libby's preference. She'd gotten home late, but she "had to respect" what she knew was a strategic moment for her daughter Elly, a chance to learn and grow.

Libby watched her bake the cake and then make a mistake, putting an egg in the frosting because she'd misread the instructions. Practicing what she calls "mastery of emotions" from her training in theater, Libby recognized that here was something her nine-year-old daughter needed to learn. At the appropriate time, she handed her another box of frosting mix and watched Elly bring the process to completion, decorating the cake and beaming with accomplishment.

The cake was so pretty the family decided to save it to enjoy the next day. But that afternoon, the family dog, Coco, was hit by a car. After they'd rushed their injured dog to the vet, Elly ran back into the kitchen in tears and redecorated the cake with the affirmation, "Coco lives." The next day, Libby got Coco out of the emergency hospital, which was charging an exorbitant fee, and took her to a kindly vet who set her broken leg. To everyone's relief, Coco recovered.

"There's no time off when you're a mother," Libby says. She credits her own mother, a therapist still active in her seventies, for giving her an example of competence and flexibility.

Libby actively defines for herself what it means to be a woman. "Being a woman is not being a pretend man," she says. Ultimately, each of us needs to transcend other people's assumptions and create her own personal definition of womanhood.

Libby says her colleagues kid her about being "always in motion." "I try to move as much as I can," she says. It's how she stays fit—with young children at home she can't commit to a set workout schedule, "so I move, swim, whenever I can." But, in a deeper sense, her love of movement reflects her view of life as a dynamic process.

Within this dynamic dance, Libby also finds time to treat herself. "You have to find your private moments in everything," she says. "Buy the sweet scented candle—even if it's expensive—because if you don't learn to feed yourself, you'll wither and feel angry." It's up to each of us to ask for what she needs, take charge of her life, and create her own harmony.

The *Tao* says to look:

*Beyond division*
*Find power in wholeness.*
TAO, 55

Your idea of harmony may be less polyphonic, less complex than Libby's. But beyond the differences lies an important principle: You can make your life more harmonious by approaching it as a dynamic dance among the many things you do, remaining true to your own nature in the process.

## $\mathcal{T}$HE WAY OF ONENESS IN NATURE

THE *TAO* tells us:

*When we value ourselves*
*As part of nature*
*And value nature*
*As ourselves,*
*We're at home*
*In the oneness*
*Of Tao.*
TAO, 13

Wise women have always found strength and serenity in the natural world. Hiking in the wilderness or pausing to gaze at flowers in a local park, walking in the woods to gather healing herbs, cultivating their gardens along with their souls, for centuries women have found renewal in nature. In touching nature, we touch the source of all life, gaining wisdom and strength in the process. In a recent study of older women remarkable for their vitality and accomplishment, all of them said they loved gardening and felt "a closeness with nature."[2]

Touching the earth can be tremendously healing. After days of back-to-back appointments and a morning of errands, my friend Tina rushed home feeling scattered and empty. She called her friend, postponing their afternoon appointment long enough to catch her breath. Then she went into her garden and set out six new plants. As she worked the soil with her trowel, she began to feel more relaxed. When she'd finished, she raised her eyes to the blue sky overhead and breathed a sigh of relief. The clouds of stress lifted and she felt like herself once more.

Taking a few moments to prune a bonsai tree, trim the roses, or visit with my vegetable garden gives me a similar feeling of relief and renewal. Touching the earth, whether in a forest, a garden, or a tiny bonsai returns us to the oneness of life.

GETTING IN TOUCH WITH NATURE

Remember to make time in your life to touch the earth and renew your connection with nature. Some ways to do this are:

- Take a walk in a local park. Watch the birds. Feed the squirrels. Notice the signs of life. Enjoy the colorful panorama of activity.
- Follow an ancient Buddhist practice and plant a tree. Tend it with care and watch it grow. See what lessons it teaches as it goes through nature's cycles, shedding its leaves, lying dormant, then blossoming and bearing fruit.
- Set out small pots of herbs in a sunny kitchen window. Pinch the herbs and add them to your foods. Savor their fresh aroma and flavor.

## ONENESS IN CONTEMPLATIVE RITUALS

WE CAN find oneness in the quiet tasks that heal our lives like a mantra. Traditionally, women's work was filled with simple tasks, repetitive and ritualistic—baking bread, folding laundry, ironing, and sewing.

My grandmother's kitchen was a wonderful place, with pots simmering on the stove and fragrant spices filling the air. Her hands covered with flour, she would show me how to pinch dough for dumplings and roll out the crust for one of her pies. Or we'd sit with paper bags and big bowls on our laps, snapping green beans. These tasks held a comfortable rhythm all their own. To this day, I still feel a happy nostalgia whenever I snap green beans. Many rituals from our childhood reach deep into our heart centers.

Performing such tasks, our hands are busy but our minds are free—free to sort through the bits and pieces of thoughts, weaving them together into new patterns of wholeness. Today modern machines wash our dishes and clothes, synthetic fabrics have reduced the need for ironing, frozen pies and dinners are ready in minutes in the microwave. Technology has freed up time for women to work outside the home and accomplish things our grandmothers would not have dreamed possible. But this efficiency has come at a price, the price of those simple rituals that helped us touch the depths within us.

## FINDING YOUR OWN RITUAL

ON THE edge of the twenty-first century we cannot go back to a simpler time. But we can regain a sense of wholeness by observing our own favorite rituals.

We're all involved in dozens of activities. The difference between routine and ritual is our attitude. Routine tasks are the ones we do mindlessly. They neither interest nor inspire us, so we want to put them off or get them over with as soon as possible. Ritual moments are times when life assumes greater depth and meaning because we put more of ourselves into what we're doing. By paying attention to the small things you do each day, you can develop greater mindfulness. Experience more often the sacredness of ritual moments, times when you feel a sense of oneness shining through your actions, healing and illuminating your life.

## SEEKING THE ONE

FOR ALL of us there are times when, in a moment of transcendent beauty, we see beyond the daily details of life and feel one with a larger whole. Artists and writers describe this as a flash of inspiration. Mystics call it a religious experience. Romantics feel it as intense and unifying love. Abraham Maslow called it a "peak experience," a sign of psychological health.[3] It is a time when our sense of self expands and the world embraces us in return, when all is suddenly, serenely One.

Many women experience oneness in response to nature or a beautiful piece of music. Others find communions in the commonplace. My friend Tina had a peak experience climbing the mountains of Peru. Tracey finds her communions skiing or walking in the woods. Marcia felt a sense of oneness while holding her sleeping child. Whatever the context, these moments of oneness bring us a deep sense of harmony as we see into the heart of life.

### FINDING YOUR OWN VISION OF ONENESS

What can you do to bring more of these communions into your life? What is it that makes you feel profoundly happy, free, and at peace?

- Walking in the woods?
- Meditating?
- Visiting a cathedral?
- Playing your favorite sport?
- Watching the ballet?
- Attending a concert?
- Visiting an art museum?
- Playing with your dog or cat?
- Volunteering at a local shelter?

Each of us has her own source of inspiration. Wherever you find yours, arrange to act on it as often as you can. Whatever brings you this feeling of oneness enriches your life in indescribable ways.

## $\mathcal{E}$MBRACING THE ONE

THE TAOIST principle of oneness is written in the sky, the oceans, and the landscape. It is the interrelatedness of life, the necessary fulfillment of each part for the survival of the whole. Life is a delicate balance, a living mandala, moving together in dynamic harmony.

Respect is essential, for each life is valuable. No part can be ignored or disdained without injury to the whole. As it is wrong to subjugate others, it is equally wrong to let them subjugate you. Live this vital lesson of Tao and embrace your own uniqueness as an essential part of all that is. As the *Tao* reminds us:

*The woman of Tao*
*Holds oneness in her heart*
*And her world is at peace,*
*Does not try to please*

*And therefore shines,*
*Does not seek attention*
*And therefore excels,*
*Does not justify herself*
*And is therefore trusted,*
*Does not imitate others*
*And is therefore herself,*
*Does not compete*
*And therefore no one in the world*
*Can surpass her.*
TAO, 22

■ *Practice accepting yourself at a deeper level.*

Find some quiet time for yourself to write down the answers to these questions. Take this book and a notepad or journal to a coffee shop, library, or park. Then ask yourself:

1. *Have I been feeling disconnected from part of my life? Have I been unwilling to accept*

   • Part of my body?
   • Something in my past?
   • One of my habits?

2. *How does this lack of acceptance make me feel:*

   • Ashamed?
   • Inadequate?
   • Incomplete?

3. *Is there something I can* do *about this part of my life?*

   • If it's a bad habit, what can I do to break it?
   • If it's part of my body, what can I do about it, *really:* take better care of myself, do something to improve my (hair, skin, face, or figure), accept myself for who I am?
   • If it's some part of my past, what can I do about it *now:* take some action to make amends, learn from the experience, forgive myself?

4. *Now, make a plan of positive action. Write down one thing you can do.*

5. *Visualize yourself doing what you've planned. How does this make you feel?*

6. *Take a deep breath and release it with a smile. Expand your awareness throughout your body and experience all that you are right now: a unique and valuable woman, becoming more focused, more mindful, more whole.*

7. *When you're ready, follow through with your action plan.*

■ *Practice your own ritual of oneness.*

Do you have your own contemplative ritual, a task that brings you greater peace of mind? It can be a favorite hobby—needlework, gardening, painting—or a simple task like folding laundry. Your ritual is as personal as your signature. What one woman resents as dull routine may be an act of renewal for another. My friend Peggy enjoys ironing, a chore I've always disliked.

- What is your contemplative ritual?
- Do you take time to do it regularly?
- If not, make time. Plan it into your life this week.
- You'll find how powerful this simple ritual can be, offering you regular time for reflection and renewal.

■ *Use this simple affirmation.*

The next time you feel stressed out, stop, take a deep breath, and say to yourself while breathing out:

*One.*
*I am one.*
*One.*
*One.*

You are infinitely more than what you do, more than what your family or employer wants from you at the moment. Your life is a pattern at once unique and essential to the universe.

# The Lesson of Centering

Too many bright colors

Can blind your eyes.

Too much sound

Deafen your ears,

Too much spice

Can burn your tongue.

Wanting more

Can drive us crazy.

Therefore the Tao woman

Rejects excess,

Turns from externals,

Embraces the inner wisdom.

*TAO, 12*

Women today have exciting, colorful lives, but each of us has her limits. Too many bright colors, too much noise, even too much of a *good* thing can wear you down. Too much stress can make you lose your center, your sense of who you are and what you value, throwing your life off balance.

One day a few years ago, I was pushing my own personal limits. As chair of a university English department, I had a pile up of commitments and my calendar looked like a disaster area. In the next few weeks, I had to staff all our fall courses, cope with a hiring freeze, complete all the administrative paperwork, teach my classes, meet a writing deadline, put my condominium up for sale, look for a new house, and plan my wedding. In my stack of mail was a summons for jury duty and a letter from my parents, who wanted to come up for a visit.

After a hectic morning, I joined two women friends for lunch at a nearby restaurant. As I sat down, a wave of dizziness swept over me. I tried to pretend everything was okay, but felt that I was going to pass out. I finally had to put my head on the table and admit that my world was spinning too fast to keep up. The centrifugal force of too many activities, too little sleep, and no margin for myself had made me lose not only my center but almost my consciousness.

I'd had an attack of anxiety and exhaustion, brought on by a frantic, nonstop life. Stress overload is all too common to many women today. Trying to be too many things to too many people can overtax your circuits, just as plugging too many appliances into the same outlet can blow your electrical power.

Have you been under too much stress lately? Don't wait until you blow a fuse to find out. Here are some common symptoms:

- Exhaustion and lack of energy
- Chronic anxiety, inability to relax
- Tension in your neck, upper back, chest, or jaw

- Dizziness or heart palpitations
- Ongoing digestive problems or diarrhea
- Sleep disturbances
- Loss of interest in relationships, recreation, or sex
- Lack of joy—life feels like an endless list of duties and obligations

If you've been experiencing one or more of these symptoms, you could be on stress overload. The centering lessons in this chapter will help get your life back in balance.

## TAKE CHARGE OF YOUR LIFE

THE PATH to greater peace begins when you realize that you are in charge of your life. If you feel that events around you are spinning out of control, take a deep breath, release it slowly and deliberately, and say to yourself, "I am the center of my life."

Being the center of your life does not mean ignoring your faith, your work, or those you love. It *does* mean making life's choices from a strong center of gravity, mindful of your own needs and values.

We've all been conditioned to be so altruistic, so other-directed, that we can easily forget one simple fact: Most of the "demands" other people make on you aren't really that urgent. Other people may know you, love you, "need" you, but only *you* are responsible for your life.

You are, first of all, responsible for your health. If you're experiencing physical symptoms of stress, call your doctor for a checkup. After that experience at lunch, I scheduled an appointment with my internist and saw a Chinese herbalist recommended by my friend Bonnie. Fortunately, my physical exam revealed no major medical problems, and my visit to Dr. Chu taught me some vital lessons in balance. I entered his office, looking at all the shelves on the wall, filled with jars of tea, ginseng, and mysterious dried ingredients. Dressed in a white lab coat, the doctor greeted me with a smile, taking my pulse and medical history. "How much sleep do you get?" he asked.

"Well . . ." I began.

"Not enough," he added.

"How much exercise do you get each day?"

I confessed that I'd been working too hard lately to exercise much.

"Balanced diet? Fresh vegetables?"

I thought of all the times I'd worked through lunch on deadline projects, snacking on the crackers in my desk.

The doctor shook his head. The facts were obvious. Against my own better judgment I'd been subordinating my health to an unnatural lifestyle that was both dehumanizing and debilitating.

For most of my adult life, I'd prided myself on my competence and sense of responsibility. I was always the one people could count on to get the job done. I'd been sabotaging myself with my own sense of duty, pushing my needs aside to take care of everything else. Hardly a prescription for a healthy life, this imbalanced attitude is all too common to modern women.

Dr. Chu gave me some ginseng and herb tea to replenish my *ch'i* or vital energy. But his main emphasis was living a balanced life. He told me to exercise for fifteen minutes twice a day, get more sleep, and eat more fresh fruits and vegetables. His advice seemed simple enough, but I wondered how I could find time for more sleep and exercise in my busy life. As I drove home, it dawned on me that if I'd neglected my car the way I'd been neglecting my body it would have broken down a long time ago.

## $\mathcal{G}$IVING YOURSELF MARGINS

THE NEXT morning I sat down with a pencil and paper and went over Dr. Chu's recommendations. Whenever we set new goals, we discover new possibilities. I realized I could give myself more margins, "time-outs" for rest and renewal. Now I bring healthy salads and sandwiches to work and take walks around campus at noon instead of staying at my desk. I also relax for a few minutes at the end of the day. Before beginning my evening activities, I make myself a cup of tea, kick off my shoes, play with my dog, or read—whatever I feel like doing. If I'm tired, I take a nap. And taking regular walks around the neighborhood with my dachshund, Heidi, has become an enjoyable ritual for both of us.

After just a few days, I began to feel better, physically and mentally. I could see new options where before there were only demands and obligations. Now, whenever I feel my schedule closing in on me, I remember this simple lesson: that giving myself more margins helps bring me back to center, increasing my joy, power, and peace of mind.

## $\mathcal{F}$INDING YOUR CENTER

WE LOSE our centers when we subordinate ourselves to our jobs, projects, or relationships. Living with greater power and peace means recognizing the real center of your life.

While people in the Western world define their directions as north, south, east, and west, in China there are *five* directions: north, south, east, west, and *center*—the Chinese character *zhong* that begins this chapter. Modern women who find themselves pulled in four directions at once need to remember this fifth direction, the center that holds our lives together. Being centered means staying in touch with yourself at a deeper level, becoming more aware of your own energies, values, and priorities. You can become more centered by taking time for yourself regularly. That way you won't get so caught up in outside activities that you forget who you are.

## CENTERING AND CHOICES

CENTERING IN on our priorities, we make conscious choices instead of mindlessly subordinating ourselves to external demands. Like a Chinese restaurant, each day is filled with many possibilities. But we cannot order everything on the menu—kung pao shrimp, almond chicken, sweet and sour pork, chow mein, lo mein, egg foo yung, egg rolls, fried rice, steamed rice, and rice noodles. There is only so much room on your plate, only so much time in a day.

Saying yes to one possibility means saying no to others, at least for today. Following the Tao of Womanhood means acknowledging priorities, honoring what you value most, and saying no to the rest.

## THE POWER OF SAYING NO

SAYING NO is a powerful practice, essential for personal balance and peace of mind. A healthy life requires both *yin* and *yang*, yes and no. Yet many of us hate to say no. Unwilling to disappoint people or hurt their feelings, we diminish ourselves instead, complicating our lives with unwanted obligations.

Saying no is warrior work, the inner martial art that helps you live more authentically. Like the women samurai of old Japan, you can cut through the unessential with the inner sword of your intention. Learning to say no without guilt will reduce the stress in your life, giving you time for what you truly value.

LIKE ANY art, saying no takes practice. There are different kinds of nos and some are more difficult than others. But with each no to someone else, we say yes to ourselves and our own values.

There are the dramatic nos when we affirm our own integrity. A few years ago, Karen worked as a research toxicologist investigating the health effects of tobacco. She was asked to perform tests to help a major tobacco company project a positive image. When her research showed how toxic the product really was and the company wanted to discount her findings, she resigned in protest.

There are also the small everyday nos that don't seem like much by themselves, but together they're the emotional calisthenics that build our personal power. When I lived in Los Angeles, I always admired Pat, a woman with the discipline to say no to social invitations, lunches with friends, even phone calls, when finishing a book. She'd tell us when she had a deadline, then keep to her word. While the rest of us were still in grad school, Pat was writing her second novel. Saying no to distractions helped her say yes to her goals.

## SAYING NO AS A MARTIAL ART

Martial artists often punctuate their kicks or punches with a powerful *kiai*, a shout that cuts through the air like a sword, focusing their energy and stunning their opponents. If you've been having trouble saying no, try this exercise.

- Stand in a relaxed posture with your knees slightly bent and your feet about eighteen inches apart.
- Breathe into your center or *hara,* the point about two inches below your navel that aikido masters call your center of power.
- Breathe out, releasing tension. Repeat this until you feel fully present.
- Now, with a smile, thrust your left hand out in front of you, saying out loud, "yes," following with your right hand, saying, "no."
- Alternate "yes" and "no" with "no" becoming progressively louder.

Feel the power of "no," realizing, in a visceral sense, that for every "yes" there *must* be a corresponding "no." You are the center of decision in your life. "Yes" and "no" are part of the dynamic rhythm of existence.

Do this training as part of your regular exercise routine. Then each day become more mindful of saying no to small things, striking a better balance between the *yin* of agreement and the *yang* of independent action. Each time you say no, you project your own *kiai,* powerfully affirming your right to choose what is really important in your life.

## ℒIVING MORE CREATIVELY

LEARNING TO say no mindfully means getting in touch with your deepest values. As long as you seek to live by other people's patterns, you will experience inner conflicts and fail to blossom. Many women look successful but are inwardly frustrated because they've let escalating responsibilities pull them away from themselves. Novelist Amy Tan said that when she was a successful business writer she often felt a nagging sense of incompleteness, realizing she was writing for other people. When she chose to write for herself, her first novel, *The Joy Luck Club*, became a best-seller.

My friend Claudia was a successful college professor who published in academic journals and spoke to professional organizations. She had a supportive husband, two children, and a lovely home in the Oakland hills. But something was missing.

Claudia's creative voice had been stifled, her energies redirected into years of academic writing while in her heart she was a poet. Slowly she began to follow her own inner direction, setting aside time to write. She joined a local writers' group and got up the courage to send some poems to literary magazines. With cultivation, her talent blossomed. Her poems began to appear in print and she was accepted into the Squaw Valley Writers' Workshop.

She returned from the workshop realizing that her vocation was creative writing. After a long talk with her husband, she took a larger step—a leave of absence from her job to enter an M.F.A. program in poetry writing.

Last year she gave a reading to her friends and colleagues. I was deeply impressed by the transformation in my friend—the power of her poetic voice, the new energy that radiated from her blue-green eyes. As she read her poems, the images took on a life of their own—the promise of ripe persimmons, the green scent of pines. One of her poems was called "Winged Clarity," filled with the joy that comes when we choose to live from our own centers, daring to be more deeply and authentically ourselves.[1]

# CENTERING ON YOUR VALUES

THE EMOTIONAL center of your life comes from your core values. In a balanced life, these values extend outward like the petals of a flower, expressing themselves in dozens of daily choices. Consciously connecting your choices to your own deepest values will give your life greater power and peace.

Our values and goals will change in the different seasons of our lives. For years, my friend Genevieve filled her days with errands, gourmet dinners, and home-baked breads for her family. She gave special luncheons for women friends and held a weekly book group at her home. When she decided, in her sixties, to study for the ministry, she had to narrow her activities to focus on her new goal. She resigned from the book group and told friends she was no longer available to give luncheons.

According to a law of physics, for every action there's an equal and opposite reaction. Changes in our lives bring about corresponding changes in the lives around us. Some of Gen's friends complained because they missed her luncheons, and without her energy, the book group fell apart. But her husband, Lyle, responded more creatively. Since Gen was in ministerial class all day Saturday, he decided to cook dinner that night. So he went to the library, checked out some cookbooks, and began to experiment. Today, Gen has her ministerial degree and Lyle has become a gourmet cook.

When we add something new to our lives, we must make room by saying no to something else. Changes inevitably bring up new possibilities. Had Gen not simplified her life, she'd never have completed her ministerial studies. Had Lyle not responded to this opportunity, he'd never have discovered that he loved to cook.[2]

# *I*DENTIFYING YOUR CORE VALUES

YOU CAN gain greater power in this season of your life by identifying your core values. For the next five days, think of five values most important to you now. Record each one in pencil on a three-by-five card—for example, "I value my health and peace of mind." Some values might involve your personal health and fitness, your spiritual life, your career, your relationships. My friend Sunny embraces the ideal of freedom, the freedom to express herself in her own way. The important thing is to define your *own* values, to get beyond the demands and expectations of others and see life through your own priorities.

If you have more than five values, that's okay, but too many can be overwhelming. Try combining some values. Are two or three really part of a larger whole? Each day look at your cards and revise them to make your statements more precise.

### PUTTING VALUES INTO ACTION

At the end of five days, go over your cards and see how you're doing. Try to match up each value with at least one action you took this week. If you value your health, did you give yourself nutritious food, rest, and exercise? If you value peace of mind, did you set aside time for contemplation and renewal? If you don't take action to support your values, they will remain only wishful thinking.

As you put your values into action, don't overcommit. If you haven't been exercising regularly, embarking on marathon training is hardly realistic. Begin with small steps: a daily walk around the neighborhood, for example. You can always do more later. Too much too soon is a recipe for failure. The *Tao* tells us, "The journey of a thousand miles begins with a single step."

Ask yourself whether you are ready to *live* each value. If so, think of some positive actions you can take next week. If you'd like to advance in your career, join a professional organization to learn about new developments and update your résumé. If you'd like to spend more time with your family, think of some ways to do this. One busy couple I know, Jean and Bob, would put their loose change into a jar in their room. Then each Sunday after church, Jean would use that money to take one of her three children to lunch. Each week, a different child had a chance to spend some special time with her. This practice helped Jean and her children catch up on important issues and nurture their relationships.

### DAILY PRACTICE

Once you've written your values and actions on the cards, look them over every morning as you plan your day. The more we exercise conscious choice, the less we're swept along by the demands and expectations of others. We are exercising power and gaining peace.

Each morning ask yourself if your plans reflect your deepest values. Have you allowed time to do what's most important to you? If not, take charge. Remember to leave margins. If your schedule looks too crowded, move some errands to another day. Reschedule that long lunch with a friend to give yourself time to exercise. And try not to feel guilty. A real friend will appreciate your honesty. The more your daily choices reflect your core values, the more peace of mind you'll experience.

One way to identify your most important activities is to

label them. Hyrum Smith, who developed the Franklin Quest Planner, recommends that we review our personal values daily and prioritize our activities by these values. Thus, an action central to your values would be an A, something less important a B, and something relatively unimportant a C. This is an incredibly helpful practice. Label each action A, B, or C according to how important it is to you—notice that I said to *you*, not to your boss, your mother, or your next door neighbor. One person's A may well be another person's C—these are *your* choices.

Now, as you go through your day, concentrate on doing the A's first, then the B's, and, if you have time, the C's. At the end of the day, you'll experience greater satisfaction because you'll have done the things *you* value instead of mindlessly reacting to another list of obligations.[3]

I've found the three-by-five-card system a wonderful reminder. To my original five cards, I add a card every time a new challenge comes up. Instead of worrying about a problem, I rephrase my concern in a positive way. For example, if I'm worried about completing a project at work, I write, "The _____ is successfully completed. Everything I need to accomplish this is mine now." Shift your focus from worry to what you *want*, and not only will you become more centered but your powerful unconscious mind will move you in the right direction, toward the information and individuals you'll need to accomplish your goals.

## FINDING PEACE AND RENEWAL AT HOME

MANY OF us lose our centers when we lose our sense of home. Traditionally, home has been our sanctuary, a place to heal and renew ourselves, to sit on the porch on a summer evening or curl up by the fire on a cold winter night. Home is where you live, relax, regain your center, and are most fully yourself, either with those you love or in moments of solitude. But for too many people, home has become only a service station, a place to refuel before dashing off again.

At the end of a long day at work, too many women come home to a "second shift" of household chores that keeps them working nearly around the clock. In our quest for achievement, many of us have lost our sense of home. Henry David Thoreau said, "Our life is frittered away by detail. . . . Simplify, simplify"[4]—and he wrote this in 1854, in a world without cars, telephones, television, computers, E-mail, fax machines, and the thousands of errands women have inherited. How much more of a challenge it is for us to maintain our centers.

### MAKING A HOME FOR YOURSELF

Begin now to explore ways to feel more "at home" and centered.

- *Set aside a time and place each day where you can truly feel at home.* Make your own Tao space in a room of your own, a favorite corner, a comfortable chair, a place where you won't be disturbed. Tell your family or roommates that you need time to unwind. Take this time for yourself, even if only half an hour, at the beginning or end of the day. Get comfortable. Take a deep breath and slowly release it. Feel your tension gradually fall away as you rediscover the feeling of being deeply at peace.

- *Establish a ritual to mark the boundary between home and the outside world.* Susan, a busy professional woman, makes a conscious effort to relax with her family at the end of the day. She considers this "sacred time" and will not take phone calls after sundown, reserving this time for herself, her husband, and their young son. One couple I know makes it a point to leave their shoes—and the problems of the world—outside. When they step into their living room, they enter a separate space.

How can you make your home a sanctuary, a place to center and renew yourself? Try not to bring work home every night, and when you do, give yourself some time to unwind before picking up that project. Take a shower when you get home, washing away the cares of the world, and slip into comfortable clothes. Do yoga stretches. Let yourself relax. You're home.

- *Make time to enjoy yourself at home.* Sometimes we spend so much time maintaining our home that we forget to enjoy it. One couple I know has a beautiful yard but rarely spend any time outside except when they're caring for it. Celebrate life with an evening meal out on the deck or share a glass of wine at sundown. Enjoy your morning coffee in the garden every morning, not just on weekends. Make time for a romp on the lawn with your children, have a picnic in the yard or eat popcorn by the fire. Simple pleasures like these are powerful: They center you.

Look around each day for simple ways to enjoy your life and feel more at home in your world. These experiences will remind you that you are here not merely to work but to love and celebrate life.

ONE POWERFUL way to become more centered is through your diet. We've all been warned about the perils of sugar, red meat, fats, and processed foods. But instead of a negative approach, *avoiding* certain foods and feeling deprived, you can increase your energy and peace of mind by selecting more powerful foods from the samurai diet of old Japan.

In medieval Japan, samurai warriors were known for their courage and endurance, their ability to stay centered in times of crisis. Samurai women as well as men trained in the martial arts, learned to use the sword and dagger. And some of their legendary power was derived from their diet.

Even now, the Japanese have the longest life expectancy on the planet, the lowest rates of cancer and heart disease— as long as they follow their traditional diet. When they start eating more Western foods, their medical problems escalate. The samurai diet was extremely nutritious. Until the 1500s, samurai ate no meat or fried foods, only seafood, fresh vegetables, brown rice, whole-wheat noodles, tea, and soy products, prepared with simple elegance.

Your own version of the samurai diet will increase your stamina, regulate your hormone levels, and lower your risk of heart disease, cancer, and premature aging. Start eating like a samurai by gradually adding more of these powerful foods to your meals until they become a natural part of your life.

*Complex carbohydrates: the most efficient source of energy for the body.* The samurai ate brown rice, bean sprouts, and wheat noodles. You can eat the same, as well as pasta, wheat, corn, oats, other whole grains, and beans. Gradually work up to three to five servings of these powerful foods a day. Enjoy whole-wheat cereal or toast for breakfast, brown rice or pasta with lunch or dinner. Add cooked beans, bean sprouts, or pasta to salads, and have rice cakes or popcorn as snacks.

*Garlic and onions: natural antitoxins.* The samurai enjoyed these as seasonings and condiments. Both foods from the allium family have natural antibiotic and antifungal properties. Garlic has been shown to reduce the risk of cancer and lower cholesterol, preventing heart disease. Add garlic and onions to soups, sauces, garnishes, and stir-fried dishes.

*Omega-3 fish oils: for lower cholesterol and a stronger immune system.* The samurai enjoyed fish grilled, baked, steamed, stir-fried, and raw as sashimi. Medical research has found that salmon, trout, halibut, mackerel, bluefish, herring, shad, butterfish, pompano, tuna, and sardines contain omega-3 oils, which lower cholesterol, reduce inflammation, and strengthen our immune systems. Gradually work some of these fish into your diet two or three times a week.

*Yams and soy products: natural plant estrogens.* Both foods help regulate women's menstrual cycles, reducing or eliminating PMS, sleep disturbances, mood swings, hot flashes, and other effects of menopause. Add yams to your diet by slicing them into stir-fry dishes. Sprinkle slices with cinnamon and cook them in the microwave, or bake them like potatoes. Japanese women, who eat soy regularly, have no word in their language for hot flashes and rarely get breast cancer. Like the samurai, they still use soy in many forms—boiled, steamed, baked, fermented, liquefied, and made into a paste.

Tofu is one easy-to-use soy food. The color and consistency of egg whites, it blends with a variety of different flavors. Rich in calcium, it lowers cholesterol, helps prevent osteoporosis and many forms of cancer. You can buy tofu in the vegetable section of your market and keep it in your refrigerator in a container of fresh water. Use it in stir-fry dishes. Slice it on top of soups and salads.

*Fresh fruits and vegetables: rich in vitamins, minerals, fiber, and antioxidants.* The samurai ate fresh greens, bean sprouts, seaweed, and fresh fruit. You can improve your health by eating fresh fruits and vegetables five times a day. It's not really that complicated: orange juice or fresh fruit for breakfast, a salad at lunch or dinner, apples or bananas as snacks, and fresh vegetables with dinner.

All vegetables are rich in vitamins and fiber. Cruciferous vegetables—broccoli, cabbage, Brussels sprouts, asparagus, kale, and cauliflower—are great anticarcinogens. Most of these vegetables are delicious steamed in the microwave. Just put them in a covered dish with a tablespoon of water and a dash of your favorite herbs or spices. Cook on high for three minutes or until done al dente. (Microwave cooking times vary with the power of the oven.) In your salads, add sliced cabbage or bean sprouts for extra fiber and raisins for extra iron.

Fresh fruits contain vitamins and antioxidants, which strengthen our immune systems and combat free radicals, preventing degenerative diseases and premature aging. Keep a basket of fruit in your kitchen for snacks and desserts. Eat apples and bananas year-round. Bring a different fruit home from the grocery store each week and discover your own favorites. Strawberries are delicious and filled with vitamin C. Slices of melon are cool and easy summer desserts. Berries make great toppings for waffles or pancakes.

*Tea: rich in antioxidants.* The samurai found peace of mind in the tea ceremony. Buddhist monks have used tea for centuries as part of their meditative practice. Both black and green tea reduce cholesterol. Their antioxidants break down free radicals, preventing cancer and gum disease. Enjoy a cup of tea with meals or as a welcome break during the day.

*A good vitamin/mineral supplement.* The samurai faced many challenges, but not the stress of pollution and the pace of modern living. Because of stress, pollution, and the soil depletion that reduces the vitamins and minerals in today's foods, nutritionists recommend vitamin supplements to our diets.

Christiane Northrup, M.D., holistic gynecologist and founder of Women to Women health practice in Yarmouth, Maine, recommends that we add to our diet a daily vitamin supplement of:

Vitamin C (500–1000 mg)
Beta-carotene (15,000–25,000 iu)
B complex (50–100 mg of $B_1$, $B_2$, $B_3$, $B_5$, and $B_6$; 75–400 mcg of $B_{12}$)
Folic Acid (200–800 mcg)
Vitamin D (200–400 iu)
Vitamin E (200–400 iu)
Selenium (100–200 mcg)
Calcium (1,000 mg)

along with the following minerals:

Magnesium (400–800 mg)
Chromium (100–200 mcg)
Manganese (5–15 mg)
Iron (10–30 mg) (during periods)[5]

*Water: the source of all life.* The poetry of the *Tao* celebrates the power of water for its strength and inspiration. You can use this power to cleanse your body from within, improve your skin tone, and stabilize your weight by drinking two quarts of water a day. Keep a favorite water bottle or glass with you and reach for it often.

With the samurai diet, as with any new endeavor, the wisest way is to start slowly. Begin drinking more water and eating more of these powerful foods until they become a regular part of your life. For greater balance, select different foods from the wide variety of choices in each category. Soon you'll begin to feel more centered, facing each day with greater vitality and confidence.

■ *Center in on your health.*

Has your life become too hectic? Start taking some regular "time-outs" to renew yourself.

- *Make your lunch hour a real break.* Get away from your desk. My friend Judy brings her walking shoes to work and takes a half-hour walk during lunch. In the past ten months she's gradually lost over seventy pounds, lowered her cholesterol, and improved her stamina and peace of mind. She looks years younger and has become a fitness role model to her friends.[6]
- *When the weather's bad and you can't go outside during lunch, you can still take a time-out.* Close your door, turn off your phone, put up a DO NOT DISTURB sign, and give yourself that hour to get back in touch with yourself. Put your feet up and close your eyes; let your mind go blank and focus on your breathing as you relax into meditation. Write a letter to a friend or read a favorite book.
- *Take regular breaks.* If you work with a computer, prevent carpal-tunnel syndrome and eyestrain by looking away from the screen, getting up periodically to walk across the room or get a drink of water. If you work at home, give yourself short breaks as well.
- *Meet a friend for workouts or sign up for an exercise class together.* Making time for exercise is easier when we include a commitment to a friend. Lots of women jog in pairs. It's safer,

and your commitment to each other reinforces your commitment to exercise. We'll often do something for a friend we wouldn't do for ourselves. My friend Janette and I once signed up for a Saturday morning ballet class at the YWCA. Many mornings I wouldn't have gotten up for class had Janette not been waiting for me.

- *Take out your knitting or needlepoint.* Many women find the regular rhythm of needlework clears their minds and refreshes them like a meditation as they watch the colorful yarns take shape in beautiful patterns.
- *Add more fun to your schedule.* Do you have a task you *have* to do—working on a big report for work, cleaning your house, polishing the furniture? Complement that tough task with something you enjoy. Give yourself a treat—a trip to your favorite bookstore, park, or movie—*after* you complete a major portion of the report. Listen to music or watch a favorite video while cleaning or polishing the furniture.
- *Give yourself something to look forward to each day.* Meet a friend for coffee, schedule a massage or facial, take a bubble bath, listen to your favorite music, read a new book, or just relax. Think of whatever renews you and *do* it regularly.

■ *Centering Practices to Remember:*

- Make yourself a place to feel "at home."
- Center in on good nutrition.
- Live your core values in the choices you make each day.

惯

# The Lesson of Compassion

Through detachment
We see the larger patterns.
Through compassion
We perceive the particulars.
Their source is the same
Though they differ in name,
The mystery of life,
The infinite Tao.

*TAO, 1* [1]

## A LESSON FROM QUAN YIN

Every culture has its legends, its archetypes, its symbols of loving-kindness. Quan Yin is the Chinese goddess of compassion.

When I was a child, I used to love looking at the white porcelain figurine of Quan Yin in my parents' living room. She stood in long, flowing robes on a base of lotus blossoms, her arms outstretched in a gesture of compassion. Her lovely face was as serene as a Buddha's, her smile filled with infinite love. Just looking at her made me feel more peaceful.

My mother had gotten the statue in Hong Kong and told me why one of its tiny hands was removable, molded from a separate piece of porcelain. As the goddess of compassion, Quan Yin's love is always available. Her hand could be removed by anyone, symbolizing her infinite generosity, for Quan Yin offers "a helping hand" to all.

That hand was lost during one of my family's many moves, a fact that always troubled me, so much so that I once carved a new hand for her out of Ivory soap. It was a poor substitute for the original but it pained me to see the beautiful goddess of compassion sadly bereft and incomplete.

Our compassion, too, is incomplete if it excludes ourselves. Reaching out to give from our hearts is beautiful. An expression of our deepest humanity, true compassion not only nurtures others, it brings our own lives greater meaning, purpose, and power.[2] But giving with resentment, acting out of guilt or obligation, only drains and depletes us. Exhausting our resources, giving ourselves away, we soon have nothing left.

The logic of this is powerfully clear, but our cultural conditioning often makes us feel far otherwise. Too many of us get caught up in the habit of mindless giving, giving because it's expected of us, or giving from a sense of inferiority—doing favors, making ourselves indispensable so others will love us. We can bring greater power and peace to our lives by practicing more complete compassion.

Eleanor Roosevelt's courage and compassion led her through a series of personal crises to fulfillment in a life of public service. A model for Abraham Maslow's concept of self-actualization, she brought inspiration to thousands struggling with the darkness of the Great Depression and the chaos of a world at war. Overcoming personal challenge and political criticism, she developed her own powerful motto, "No one can make you feel inferior without your consent."[3]

Living a compassionate life always begins with you. It means reaching out to others as the unique individual you are, never allowing anyone to make you feel inferior. It means respecting your needs, your body, and your own unique spirit, transcending the limiting judgments of others to become more powerfully, more peacefully, yourself.

## $\mathcal{C}$OMPASSION AS *AHIMSA*

*AHIMSA*, THE principle of compassion practiced by Buddhists and Hindus, means *living in a way that causes no harm to any living being.* My Buddhist friends Sunny and Miki are vegetarians to avoid harming animals. *Ahimsa* also means avoiding harm to other human beings, relating to them with kindness and respect, regardless of their behavior. The principle of *ahimsa* inspired Gandhi's ideal of nonviolence, which treated all persons, even enemies, with profound compassion.

This chapter will help you extend the healing power of *ahimsa* to yourself as well as others, overcome old habits of compliance, make peace with your body, and live with greater wholeness and integrity.

### AHIMSA AND ALTRUISM

All too often, women apply *ahimsa* to everyone but ourselves. We care for others in countless ways—running errands, returning calls, listening to problems, saying yes to too many social obligations. But our compassion is incomplete.

Responding to requests for our time and energy, unwilling to hurt people's feelings, we fill up our days until we have nothing left. In practicing kindness to others we are often *unkind* to ourselves.

What looks like admirable, caring behavior can become a destructive habit that undermines our health and peace of mind. Psychologist Carol Gilligan has pointed out the ironic contradiction in women's altruism which upholds the importance of personal care yet denies it to ourselves. She asks, "If it is good to be responsive to people, to act in connection with others and to be careful rather than careless about people's feelings and thoughts, empathic and attentive to their lives, then why is it 'selfish' to respond to yourself?"[4]

The healthy practice of *ahimsa* is not mindless self-sacrifice but loving-kindness, a reverence for life in all its varied forms. And one of those forms is you.

## *E*XPERIENCING COMPASSION

THE CONCEPT of complete compassion is hard to grasp. Many of us are more familiar with what it is *not*. But as the *Tao Te Ching* tells us:

> *Heaven and earth join together*
> *And the sweet rain falls*
> *Equally on all*
> *In natural harmony.*
> TAO, 32

Compassion is the spirit of caring that connects all of life, the closeness of comfort and security, the warmth of a good relationship, the kind gesture of a friend. It is both *yin* and *yang,* giving freely from the heart and accepting in our hearts the beauty around us. Known by many names—*agape, caritas, ahimsa* are only a few—compassion is a guiding principle in the major world religions, creating, inspiring, nurturing, and—with a power greater than we know—supporting the life on this planet.

My friends Sunny and Miki have taught me a great deal about compassion. They live simply, recycle, respect the environment, and talk about doing everything "with heart." When they opened their aikido dojo in Fremont, California, their generous spirits transformed a vacant warehouse into a heartwarming training hall that renews people in body and soul.

I have a photo of them the day they moved in, with tools and layers of Sheetrock stacked against the wall. Tall, blond, and muscular, Sunny stands beside Miki. Graceful as a dancer, with her long black hair pulled back in a braid, she smiles at this new beginning that echoes the traditions of her samurai ancestors. Together with their friends, the couple remodeled and painted, creating a martial arts training hall that looks more like a Buddhist temple—spacious, white, and serene, with beautiful calligraphy hanging on the walls, a carefully swept white canvas mat, and green plants bringing a touch of nature inside. For the first year, each time I came to train at the dojo, I noticed another touch of beauty— a new plant by the door, a new painting, Miki's artistry with dried flowers. They installed a small pond and fountain, filling the dojo with the healing sounds of water and the beauty of golden koi encircled by a grove of tropical plants.

But the transformation was more than physical. Unlike some martial arts schools, where people become competitive and aggressive, theirs has become like an extended family, developing compassion among all its members. A spirit of mutual encouragement includes everyone from the youngest child to the oldest adult, and the dojo has evolved into a community center with potluck parties, food donations over the holidays, and neighborhood outreach projects.

For everyone from the newest student to the most advanced black belt, aikido has become a way to "polish our spirits," open our hearts, and learn more about ourselves. Our training combines the energies of *uke*, the person who attacks, and *nage*, the one who executes the technique. We alternate roles, taking turns being *uke* and *nage*. Joyously extending our energies in a partnership of give-and-take, we learn as much by attacking as by receiving, by throwing another as by tumbling head-over-heels across the mat.

Training at the dojo has taught me that compassion is more than a one-way street. In life, as in aikido, there's a natural rhythm of giving and receiving. When we give out of obligation or find ourselves doing all the giving in a relationship, our energies are depleted. But when we give freely from the heart, we, too, are enriched and empowered by the act of giving. Complete compassion demands courage, not only the courage to give freely but the courage to open our hearts and receive, becoming vulnerable enough to accept life's gifts instead of feeling we must work hard for everything. At the dojo I find that living with compassion is an ongoing process of discovery, of daring to live more authentically, care more deeply, know myself more fully, and celebrate life with greater reverence, in all its transformations.[5]

## $\mathcal{S}$HADOWS IN YOUR LIFE: REMOVING BLOCKS TO COMPASSION

WHETHER IN dynamic interaction or moments of stillness, compassion deepens our awareness, increasing our peace and personal power. Yet many of us cannot extend compassion to ourselves because we've let self-defeating behaviors cast their shadows across our lives. These patterns are all around us. Just listen.

Marian has a constant stream of bad luck. She didn't get a promotion at work because another woman sabotaged her. The contractors took too long to finish the addition to her house. Her car is always breaking down. And when she gets her hair done, it's never right. But instead of taking positive action—telling her supervisor, contractor, mechanic, or hairdresser what she *wants*—she complains endlessly to her friends, blaming others, reinforcing her own sense of powerlessness. Unlike Marian, Julie always blames herself. But she, too, feels powerless. When her boyfriend gets depressed, she's sure it's her fault. When a student in her class flunks a test, she's the one who feels like a failure. Her shoulders slump, her energies collapse, and she retreats from life in apologies and self-accusations.

Cynthia undercuts her credibility with friends and co-workers by prefacing all her remarks with "I know this is a dumb question, but . . ." or "This idea probably won't work but . . ." She broods endlessly, dwelling on every mistake, feeling inadequate because her performance is less than perfect.

Do some of these self-defeating patterns sound familiar? They're all signs of self-sabotage, barriers to compassion.

### EXTENDING COMPASSION TO YOURSELF

Here are some ways you can drive away the shadows of self-defeating behavior. Each day look for ways to practice *ahimsa*, being consciously kinder to yourself, giving yourself the respect you'd extend to a cherished friend or family member.

- *Do you spend time blaming yourself or others when things go wrong?* Shaming and blaming not only keep you from solving problems, they undermine your self-respect, whether the person you blame is yourself or someone else. Blaming yourself makes you feel like a loser. Blaming others makes you feel like a victim. *Ahimsa* means looking beyond blame to seek greater understanding—of yourself, the other person, and the situation. Be kinder to yourself. Stop shaming and blaming. Instead of fixating on the problem, look for the solution.

  For the past few months, Lisa had begun her days running late, feeling uncentered and resentful. Sharing a small apartment with her new husband had changed her daily routine, preventing her from exercising, dressing, and putting on her makeup as efficiently as in her old apartment. Each morning she'd wait for Ben to get out of the shower, then dash around, barely pulling herself together in time for work. Looking beyond blame for solutions, she shared her concerns with him and he got up a few minutes earlier, showered, and then made coffee for them while Lisa took her shower. She began exercising after work and laying out her clothes the night before. Suddenly mornings were more manageable and Lisa felt like herself again.

- *Do you find yourself catering to others' needs while neglecting your own?* Complete compassion means striking a better balance. Stop neglecting yourself and feeling unworthy. Remember that compassion includes you. Be kinder to yourself. Stop treating yourself as "less than."

  Betty was feeling frustrated and scattered, afraid her memory was failing because her life was filled with unfinished projects. At home and at work, the pattern was the same. Her boss, coworkers, husband, and children had all

developed the habit of interrupting her.
Mommy . . . Honey," they'd call and she'd dro
was doing to comply. When she started treat
with more respect and letting them know *wh*
available, Betty began to feel more whole, less frazzicu aim
resentful. Her memory also improved.

- *Do you put yourself down when talking to others?* This week, listen to the women you know. Notice how often they criticize themselves. How does it sound? Now listen to yourself. If you've been prefacing your remarks with "This is probably a dumb idea, but . . ." or criticizing your appearance, get a friend to help you break the habit. Agree to tell each other when you put yourselves down. Remember, *ahimsa* means treating yourself with greater respect. Be kinder to yourself. Stop self-deprecating.

- *Do you seek others' approval in order to feel okay or do things only to avoid hurting people's feelings?* Like Louise, many of us cater to others' demands because we don't want to be rude. Her neighbors, a retired couple, call or drop by every night when she comes home. After a busy day working in sales, the last thing she wants is to make small talk with neighbors. But like Louise, most of us were taught to be polite. So we accept social invitations when we'd rather stay home, wearing ourselves down trying to please others.

The next time you really *don't* feel like getting together with friends or family, try blending kindness with honesty. Say no—with compassion—"Thank you for thinking of me, but I'm really busy right now." "I'd love to, but this is not a good time for me"—and propose an alternative. *Ahimsa* means respecting your own needs as much as those of others. Be kinder to yourself about your commitments.

When you relate more out of choice than obligation, your relationships will become more authentic and your life more balanced.

## *H*AVING COMPASSION FOR YOUR BODY

WOMEN WOULD experience *far* more peace of mind if we practiced compassion for our bodies. Most of us routinely block *ahimsa* for ourselves in this important area. The *Tao Te Ching* tells us:

> *When some are called beautiful,*
> *The rest are seen as ugly.*
> *When we prize one quality as good,*
> *The rest becomes inferior.*
>
> *Yet each extreme complements the other.*
> *Large and small,*
> *Light and dark,*
> *Short and tall,*
> *Youth and age*
> *Bring balance to life.*
> TAO, 2

Throughout history women have been at war with their bodies, fighting nature to conform to artificial ideals. For centuries, Chinese court ladies were prized for their delicate beauty. Their feet, or "golden lilies," were bound in childhood to keep them forever small. The ideal size was three inches long, the ideal shape a new moon. Painfully striving for this ideal, generations of Chinese women hobbled about on feet too small to support their adult weight. Mothers began binding their daughters' feet when they were five and the painful practice continued until the revolution in the 1940s.

The Western world also prized fragile femininity, admiring women for their tiny waists. In the 1800s many women nearly starved themselves and were laced into corsets so tight they found it hard to breathe. Some women even had their lower ribs removed, all in the name of beauty.

As we approach the twenty-first century, are we any better off? How difficult it is to make peace with our bodies when fashion magazines routinely adorn teenage girls with dramatic makeup and designer clothes, holding them up as icons for adult women. It's hard to be a natural woman when magazines are filled with ads for makeup, false eyelashes, breast enhancers, artificial fingernails, wigs, and hair extensions. Daily life, for many, has become a costume drama.

## Exercising compassion for your body: taking positive action

A HEALTHY diet, exercise, and the desire to look our best are part of a balanced life. But many women become compulsive about their appearance, developing what psychologists call "dysmorphic disorder," extreme anxiety about their bodies. They obsess about apparent flaws, spend hours before the mirror, and hide under layers of makeup and baggy clothes. While most of us do not go to this extreme, recent studies have indicated that nearly all women are unhappy with the way we look.[6] Here are some ways to begin making peace with your body:

- *Stop playing the competitive game with other women.* You know what I mean—judging yourself and others by how well you measure up to some artificial standard. Self-deprecating remarks about your own appearance, envious or critical remarks about others, all fall into this category.

- *Find at least one feature you like about yourself* —your eyes, your hair, your smile, your hands—and celebrate it. Accentuate your beautiful eyes, enjoy styling your hair, smile more, treat yourself to a manicure. Begin appreciating your own beauty and uniqueness.

- *Begin to reframe the way you think about your body.* Instead of merely an object to decorate for others, see your body as a dynamic expression of who you are. My friend Catherine took up weight training and began to think of her body as a friend, developing a stronger, more assertive self.

- *Engage in action, not reaction.* Instead of focusing on imperfections, get your body moving. Meet a friend for a game of tennis, go for a swim, sign up for a dance or Jazzercise class. Or put on your favorite music and exercise in your living room. The improved circulation and endorphins from regular aerobic exercise will help put everything into better perspective.

Defining beauty as strength rather than fragile perfection can change the way we feel about ourselves. In 1996, 3,800 women competed in the Summer Olympics. Only a century ago in 1896, no women were in the Olympics at all. *The New York Times* reported that women athletes have produced a new ideal of strength and competence for women.[7] Instead of focusing on how we look to others, admiring the media icons, the stick-thin fashion models or voluptuous sex goddesses, more of us are enjoying our own workouts, reclaiming our bodies for ourselves.

Marlene Bjornsrud has spent the last twenty years playing competitive tennis, coaching professionals, and working as a college athletic director. At Grand Canyon University in Arizona, she found that women athletes respond better to *positive* coaching, words that emphasize our strength, competence, and self-respect. "Affirmation and praise go a lot farther than criticism and negatives," she says. Now she tells her coaches to "create a positive environment, couching even constructive criticism in a positive tone."[8]

You can become a better coach to yourself by being more positive in your own inner dialogue. Instead of the self-accusations and self-doubts most of us play in our heads, build your confidence by talking to yourself the way a good coach would: "Good move." "That's the way." "It's okay; you'll get it next time." "You can do it." Try it. With more compassionate coaching, you'll find your spirits soar and your performance improves.

## NURTURING WITH WISDOM AND COMPASSION

WE *ALL* need nurturing. It's part of living a compassionate life. Complete compassion means nurturing ourselves regularly and reaching out to others with our minds and hearts. Most of us nurture others automatically, but we don't always do it mindfully. Responsible nurturing means relating out of love, not obligation, balancing compassion with detachment and discernment.

Detachment prevents you from getting too emotionally caught up in a problem. By combining detachment with compassion, you can stay centered, respond effectively, and maintain perspective, which the person you're nurturing may have lost.

*Right attitude* means recognizing that you are *not* responsible for solving all the problems around you. No one is. But sometimes in our desire to be helpful we forget this. One human being can do only so much.

You can develop greater discernment the next time someone comes to you with a problem by asking yourself:

- Is this a problem I can deal with?
- What else is going on in my life right now?
- Do I have the necessary skills? What can I do within reason?

Recognizing the limits of your skills, time, and energy will keep you from being swept into an impossible tidal wave or making the other person believe you can do more than you actually can. If you lack the time or skills to solve the problem, give whatever help you can, then refer the person to someone more qualified—a therapist, tax accountant, mechanic, or doctor. The important thing is to relate with wisdom and compassion—for the other person *and* yourself.

*Right action* means recognizing the difference between a real emergency and sloppy living. An emergency mobilizes us with an instant adrenaline rush. We care, we're concerned, we want to help, so we drop everything to rush into action. But sometimes people concoct "emergencies" to manipulate us. Years ago, my boyfriend's car battery was always going dead. For weeks, he'd call saying he needed a jump start from my car. After the first time, his problem was not an emergency. It was sloppy living. He needed to buy a new battery. But he wanted to spend more time with me and knew I'd always respond to an "emergency."

If someone keeps coming to you with the same problem, it's probably not an emergency. It's just sloppy living. Look to the larger pattern. Ask yourself what's going on, who's responsible, and what this person really wants. Chances are it's not a solution as much as your attention. Recognizing the pattern can keep you from being manipulated.

## DISCERNMENT: NURTURING STRENGTH, NOT WEAKNESS

Nurturing wisely requires discernment. Despite all our good intentions, sometimes our nurturing weakens other people as well as ourselves.

Psychologists have found that we learn by reinforcement. If we reinforce behavior by giving people what they want, they'll repeat that behavior. Are you nurturing people's weakness instead of their strength?

Sheila's son Tim, age thirty-two, never seems to make it financially. Yet she's reinforced him for dependency all his life. She gave in to his pleas when he used up his allowance and wanted to buy a new toy or video game. When Tim was in college, his calls home invariably included, "Mom, I'm out of money," and she'd always send more. After graduation he moved back home until he got established. But car payments, vacations, and a new stereo system made it hard for him to live on his income, so he's been in and out of the house—and his mother's checkbook—for years. His parents would like to retire but are still waiting for their son to grow up. Until Sheila stops nurturing his weakness, Tim won't learn how to budget his money or manage his life.

Positive reinforcement encourages and perpetuates behavior. Attention is power. Whatever we give our attention to increases. When we stop reinforcing the behavior, it usually decreases or goes away. Living more compassionately means nurturing others wisely, responding to their needs *not* to perpetuate their dependency and build up our egos so we feel like superhero rescuers. True compassion encourages and empowers the people in our lives.

## PRACTICING COMPASSION AND FORGIVENESS

THE FINAL lesson in living a compassionate life is forgiving yourself and others, releasing any hurts or resentments that cast their shadows across your life. Forgiveness brings about a renewal of spirit known to Christians as the state of grace and in Chinese philosophy as *wushin*. *Wu* in Chinese means "nothingness." Combined with *shin*, the character for "heart-mind," *wushin* means literally "no mind," no ego blocks, no grudges, no prejudice. Living with *wushin* enables us to face each day without any old angers, hurts, and resentments to drain our energy and destroy our peace of mind.

### CLEANSING YOUR HEART WITH COMPASSION

You can experience *wushin* through a daily practice known as "cleansing your heart." Each night, take a few moments to review your activities, looking back on this day's unique patterns of joy and pain, *yin* and *yang*, sunlight and shadow.

- First focus on one of the shadows, a challenging moment that filled your heart with hurt, frustration, or anger. Ask yourself, "What did I learn?" "What can I do better next time?"

- Now forgive yourself and any others involved. Let the warmth of compassion embrace you, eclipsing the shadow. Draw upon your own spiritual tradition to assist you.
- Take a slow deep breath and release it, along with the experience. Feel your peace increase as the weight of emotion leaves your body.
- Now focus on one of the bright moments when you felt greater joy, power, or peace. Bask in its warmth, then ask yourself, "What did I learn?" "How can I use this insight tomorrow?"
- Take a long deep breath and let it out as you release the energies of the day in gratitude for their gifts of joy and wisdom.

Remember to end your days by cleansing your heart with compassion and gaining greater insight into life's lessons.

■ *Take some time to visualize what compassion means for you.*

How do you experience the healing power of compassion? A favorite experience for me is sitting at the beach on a sunny day, resting my back against a warm rock. The sights are a beautiful panorama—the rhythm of the waves, the sunlight on the shining water, the sea gulls circling overhead. Leaning back with my eyes closed and the sound of the waves in the background, I feel the sun's warmth soak into my body like compassion itself, removing any tension or concern. Embraced by the natural sounds and the warm, healing light, I am relaxed and at peace with the world.

What does compassion mean to you? Do you associate it with an experience in nature, a loving relationship, your religious faith? Take a few moments to reflect and focus on the feeling.

- Sit comfortably in a space by yourself and breathe into your center.
- Slowly exhale, releasing any tension.
- Take another deep breath and slowly release it. Concentrate on your breathing, feeling your body relax. Simply be present, here and now.
- Close your eyes and recall a time when you felt filled with compassion, either giving or receiving. Feel that sensation of warmth and serenity.
- Gradually return your attention to the present. Ask

yourself, "How can I experience more compassion in my life?"

- Listen to your heart, your body, your intuition. What are they telling you?
- When you are ready, return to your activities, letting the spirit of compassion guide your choices.

■ *Give yourself the gift of compassion regularly.*

Living with compassion means nurturing yourself as well as others, reaching out in ways that restore your energy and peace of mind. Here are some possibilities:

- Take a short nap after lunch or at the end of the day. Close your eyes and curl up for a few minutes of "rest period" the way you did in kindergarten.
- Take a bubble bath. Relax in the warm, sudsy water, and just *be,* emerging clean, renewed, and refreshed.
- Get a facial. Let someone else take care of you for a change.
- Get a massage. Feel the healing power of touch relax your muscles and release the tension inside.
- Soak your fingernails in warm olive oil, close your eyes, and clear your mind. This treatment will strengthen your nails and soothe your spirit.
- Go to a bookstore or library and explore, reading whatever you want.
- Give yourself a vacation in your own hometown. Get a tour book and investigate interesting places—art galleries, museums, exhibits, and good restaurants. Share your discoveries with a friend if you like.
- Call a local convent or monastery and sign up for a weekend retreat. Many welcome individuals of all

faiths for "self-directed retreats," which will give you time to read, reflect, and renew yourself, leaving the noisy world outside.

- Reach out to someone else in a spontaneous gift from the heart. Giving freely, not because you have to but because you *want* to, brings greater power and peace to both of you. Call up an old friend or send her a card. Bring someone you know fresh vegetables or flowers from your garden. Give some time to a cause you believe in. Feel your life expand with the healing power of compassion.

Whatever it is that soothes your spirit and makes you feel at peace with yourself and the world, give yourself that gift of compassion often.

■ *Remember to nurture with both wisdom and compassion.*

Have you been reinforcing someone in your life for behavior you'd rather not encourage? If so, fill in the blanks and let this exercise lead you to greater discernment.

- _____ (someone in my life) repeatedly does ____ which annoys me and I respond by _____.
- By responding in this way, have you been positively reinforcing this behavior? Are you giving the person attention or other rewards? If so, fill in the blank: I have been reinforcing him or her with _____.
- Ask, "How can I express compassion for myself and the other person *without* reinforcing the behavior?" Begin to show compassion in other ways. Give the behavior less attention.

If someone at work is always late for meetings, do

you wait for this person to arrive before starting the meeting? Don't. Start on time and don't reinforce the behavior. If your younger sister calls repeatedly asking to borrow money, next time sit down with her and help her come up with a plan to handle her finances.

- Fill in the blank: The next time _____ (the person) does _____, I will respond by _____.
- Visualize yourself practicing this new response. How does it feel?

Remember, when you change the reinforcement, the behavior will change.

SEEING THE larger patterns gives you a valuable resource to deal with life's challenges. In most cases, withdrawing reinforcement will reduce the behavior. However, if the negative behavior involves addiction, abuse, or serious psychological problems, you'll need professional help to break the pattern. But the first step in changing any behavior is awareness.

Awareness brings greater power and peace. With awareness of any pattern comes greater insight and effective action. Smile and claim this powerful new awareness for yourself.

# The Lesson of Simplicity

Only remember this:

Keep your life simple,

Your heart pure

As raw silk,

Remain whole

As uncarved wood,

Overcome

Incessant striving,

Return to center.

*TAO. 19*

There's a power in simplicity. Asian art conveys a mood of serenity with its generous use of open space. In painting and calligraphy the clear, uncluttered background is as important as the image itself. In the wide expanse of sky above a picture of Mount Fuji or the white silk paper beneath the black ink characters is what the Japanese call *yohaku,* which means literally "white space," an area deliberately left open for observers to enter.

*Yohaku* in our lives is the space of contemplation, when we slow down to listen to our hearts, gaining greater understanding and peace of mind. To experience the creative power of *yohaku*, we must learn to simplify, clearing away the clutter to establish more margins for ourselves.

Developing your own *yohaku*, you'll learn in this chapter how to balance your activities in the busy world of *yang* with the natural wisdom of *yin*, tapping the reservoir of creativity deep within you. You'll learn the discipline of *misogi*, clearing the clutter from your life to create greater peace of mind. Finally, you'll master the inner discipline of *budo*, the warrior work required to keep your life in balance.

## TAKING TIME FOR *YOHAKU*

THE ART of *yohaku* is virtually unknown to people whose days are crammed with events scheduled back-to-back. We often leave ourselves no room to reflect, missing the renewal that comes from regular margins of open time. *Yohaku* does not mean sitting in front of a TV set or killing time in mindless pursuits. It's the grace of contemplation that opens us up to a wisdom deep within.

Simply spending a few hours relaxing outside or reading seems almost unthinkable for some people. They feel compelled to *purchase* their contemplative time.

Every year Lee Ann and her husband spend Christmas in Hawaii to escape the holiday rush. There they can respectably do nothing—sit in a chair by the pool reading paperback novels or just dozing off. They can take quiet walks on the beach or watch the sunset, getting back in touch with themselves and one another. But sunsets, solitude, and those we love are available to us every day. Do we really have to spend thousands of dollars to find open time?

## THE GIFT TO BE SIMPLE

Enjoy the gift of open time regularly. Here are some ways to do this:

- *Make a standing appointment with yourself.* Write your name on your calendar this week and set aside at least an hour to do whatever you feel like at the moment as long as it's not work or errands. Get reacquainted with an old friend—yourself.
- *Give yourself wider margins between errands and appointments.* Instead of rushing from one thing to the next, you'll have a built-in "breather" to relax and collect yourself, and you'll feel more serene.
- *Take regular* yohaku *breaks with someone you love.* Take a walk around the neighborhood together. Enjoy the fresh air, slow down, and get back into the natural rhythm of walking. Exchange back rubs or foot massages. Or have coffee at a place with a view and watch the world go by. Take time to share life's simple pleasures together.

## SIMPLIFYING TO BUILD YOUR CREATIVE POWER

IT MAY feel strange to put periods of unstructured time into your busy days, but they are a valuable natural resource. For centuries, artists and innovators have known the inspiration that comes with open time. This is the "incubation" period, a crucial stage in any creative process. When we've come to an impasse and done as much as we can on a project, often the best thing to do is take a break, go for a walk, take a nap, and let the insights come.

Thomas Edison kept a cot in his laboratory and took naps when he needed new insight. Henry David Thoreau wrote from his cabin in the woods, "There were times when I could not afford to sacrifice the bloom of the present moment to any work, whether of the head or hands. I love a broad margin to my life."[1] Virginia Woolf said all women need a room of their own where they can withdraw from the world to think, write, and renew themselves. Anne Morrow Lindbergh spent time by herself at a small beach cottage, recording her lessons of peace and renewal in *Gift from the Sea*.

Take your cue from these people. Build margins for contemplation and renewal into your life. Leave room for inspiration, the quiet moments that lead to new possibilities, increasing your peace and creative power. As the *Tao* reminds us:

> *The woman who listens*
> *To her own quiet wisdom*
> *Creates harmony*
> *In her world.*
> TAO, 45

## THE POWER OF *MISOGI*

ONE RAINY day in Mendocino underscored for me the power of *misogi*, the art of eliminating the nonessential. Taking a walk around this small artists' colony on the northern California coast, I came upon a group of eight women from the Mendocino Art Center making sculptures under the redwood trees. Blending with the sounds of a gentle spring rain, the tapping of their hammers made their own kind of music as these women chipped away the nonessential, turning stone blocks into their own designs.

Designing our lives is our own personal work of art. Like the sculptors, each day, we too must chip away the nonessential, asking:

"What do I want to express?"
"What is essential to my design?"
"What do I need to chip away?"

Living the Tao of womanhood is an ongoing spiritual exercise, a path leading from preordained patterns to personal artistry, from repression to self-expression. A vital tool in becoming artists of the possible is the practice of *misogi*— clearing away whatever does not contribute to your own work of art. As the *Tao* tells us:

*When pursuing knowledge*
*Much is collected.*
*When following the Tao,*
*Much is left behind.*

*Cast away the unessential*
*To reach the essence.*
*Through simplicity*
*All that matters*
*Is accomplished.*

TAO, 48

# THE COST OF CLUTTER

By ELIMINATING needless stressors, *misogi* will bring you greater power and peace. Examples of stress caused by clutter are all around us. Last week, Suzanne was late for work because she couldn't find her keys. Lydia had to leave work early to pay her bill at the electric company, afraid her power would be cut off. She forgets to pay bills on time because they're buried under piles of papers.

Have you experienced stress because you couldn't find things? Robbing your environment of order and beauty, clutter strangles the soul. Where is *yohaku,* the creative space, when you're hemmed in by clutter in every direction: cluttered table tops, cluttered closets, a cluttered calendar, and a cluttered life? Regardless of how much Madison Avenue tries to sell you, being filled full is not the same as being fulfilled. Let there be spaces in your life to move, to breathe. Begin clearing away clutter with the powerful practice of *misogi.*

# FROM ROUTINES TO RITUALS: MAKING THE EVERYDAY SACRED

*MISOGI* IS an ancient Shinto ritual of purification. Some dedicated martial artists in Japan and America still practice *misogi harai.* Standing under a waterfall or plunging into a mountain stream in the heart of winter, they perform ritual chants, releasing discordant thought patterns to regain essential harmony.

*Misogi* for modern women means more than merely washing, cleaning house, or keeping things in order. Our attitude marks the difference between ritual and routine. Gritting our teeth in resentment, feeling enslaved by routine chores only weakens us, while Buddhist monks make their daily chores a moving meditation. Acts like chopping wood or carrying water become an extension of their contemplative practice. Performed mindfully, the simple steps of putting your life in order can become *misogi,* sacred acts, rituals of empowerment.

### PRACTICING MISOGI

You can begin a regular practice of *misogi* right now. Choose one area at a time. As you perform each task, affirm to yourself:

*"Order is a gift I give myself each day."*

- *Take charge of the paper in your life.* Recycle old magazines after you've read them. Don't let unopened mail pile up. Sort it when it comes in. Put bills in a special place, correspondence in another. Discard junk mail before it collects.
- *Eliminate clutter in the living room.* Pick up personal items when you leave the room. Before you go to bed, pick up any items left behind and put them away. If you have a family, ask them to do the same. Remember, *misogi* does not mean waiting on others. It is your gift of order to yourself. Simply clearing away clutter will make your living room a daily affirmation of beauty and peace.
- *Eliminate clutter in the bathroom.* Spend a few days organizing the bathroom. Take one task at a time. First go through the medicine cabinet, discarding outdated medications. Then look under the sink, making sure you have the necessary cleaning supplies. If you have small children

or pets, keep toxic medicines and cleaning supplies out of their reach. You may need to install child-guard locks on the cabinet doors.

Put personal-care tools—hair dryers, makeup, curling irons—away to create a clean surface. Scrub the sink and bathtub. Clean the tile grout. Polish the mirror.

Look around. If you need another towel rack, shelves, or cabinet to help you stay organized, visit a hardware store.

Bathroom *misogi* may take a week or more as you handle one part at a time, but when you're done, each morning as you brush your teeth, you'll greet the day with a greater sense of order.

• *Eliminate clutter in the kitchen.* This *misogi* will take longer. Remember, this is a ritual. Don't let it become a chore by tackling the job all at once.

Go through one drawer or cabinet at a time, putting any unnecessary items in a bag for the local donation center.

Throw away old spices and outdated items. Organize items in drawers with dividers or small boxes. Take your discards to the donation center.

Scrub the sink. Then look inside your refrigerator. Discard any outdated foods. Wipe the shelves and door. Put a box of baking soda inside to absorb odors.

Wipe down the cabinets and counters. Sweep the floor and mop it clean. Look around the room and feel a greater sense of power and efficiency.

• *Eliminate clutter in your closet.* We collect clothes and shoes to keep up with changing fashions but seldom discard the old to make room for the new. When Dora moved out of her home of twenty-five years, her closet was so packed with clothes it looked like a solid wall of fabric. In the back were dresses she hadn't worn in decades. The closet was like a calendar of bygone days with clothes stuffed in chronological layers.

Closet *misogi* will save you time dressing and give you a new wardrobe as you discover clothes you've forgotten. Remember, this is *your misogi*. No one should do closet *misogi* for anyone else for at least two good reasons: 1. *misogi* does not mean waiting on others, and 2. the faded shirt or old Levi's one person discards may be someone else's treasure.

As with the kitchen *misogi*, go through one section of the closet at a time, putting unwanted items—clothes that no longer "fit" your body, your style, your life—into a bag to give away, practicing compassion to others while you simplify your life. Discard anything you haven't worn, or are unlikely to wear, in a year—unless it's an outfit for special occasions.

Clothing can be symbolic. As you go through your closet, you'll find yourself sifting through old memories and associations. Ask yourself:

"Do I want to keep this one?"
"Am I ready to release that one?"

After eliminating the nonessential, organize your clothes by season, purpose (work clothes, sport clothes), type (suits, jackets), or color according to *your* preference. Treat yourself to new color-coordinated hangers from the drugstore. This will help inspire you and it's useful.

If you have lots of blouses, you can add an extra clothing rod to your closet. Measure your current rod and buy a wooden dowel cut to measure at the hardware store. Attach it to the clothing rod above by draping a long loop of rope or wire around each end and slipping your new dowel inside. Or attach it directly to the wall. Check out shoe racks or stackable closet organizers for sweaters and other accessories.

It may take weeks, but closet *misogi* will help you pull yourself together, body and soul. It will give you a new sense of efficiency, power, and confidence as you dress each morning.

Practicing *misogi* will bring your life greater peace and beauty. Your uncluttered surfaces, orderly bath and kitchen, and colorful, efficient closet will become a daily affirmation. Psychologist Abraham Maslow's research revealed that beauty is a basic human need and that an atmosphere of ugliness can actually make us sick.[2] Regular *misogi* will help you live a healthier life and affirm for yourself on a daily basis the reality of the old Navajo blessing,

*"May you walk in beauty."*

## 𝒯HE ART OF *BUDO:* BOUNDARY WORK

THE *TAO* tells us:

> *Maintain your boundaries,*
> *Close your door,*
> *Find the power and peace of Tao.*
> *Let down your boundaries,*
> *Open your door,*
> *And find only confusion.*
> TAO, *52*

No matter how busy you are, how many people you know and love, every healthy person needs boundaries—limits we place on our time, energies, and personal space. They enclose our inner gardens, preserving the sanctity of our souls. To paraphrase Robert Frost, good *boundaries* make good neighbors, good friends, good lives. Boundaries are not walls that close out the world. They're more like a white picket fence between your front yard and the public sidewalk, protecting the space within.

Women have a long history of neglecting their boundaries, letting others overrun their lives, like so many neighborhood dogs and cats, digging up our carefully planted flower beds. According to psychologist Jean Baker Miller, many women routinely give in to others' demands because they're afraid *not* to, afraid to risk losing love.³ But when our inner space is overrun by too many demands, we lose touch with who we are, becoming caught up in a debilitating chain of reactive behavior. A healthy life involves a dynamic give-and-take, a balance between our needs and those of others. To maintain this balance you must set boundaries.

If you've been feeling overrun, angry, or resentful lately, your emotions are telling you that something you value needs defending. It could be your boundaries, your own personal space and peace of mind. By practicing the discipline of *budo*, the way of the inner warrior, you can maintain your boundaries with awareness and positive action.

### BECOMING MORE MINDFUL OF YOUR BOUNDARIES

The first step in effective *budo* is awareness: recognizing the boundary violation. The next step is taking positive action. You can channel the energy of anger into new insight, turning frustration into liberation.

This exercise will use visualization and parody to overcome old feelings of guilt and obligation that make you cave in to others' demands. The healing power of laughter will help you break through women's traditional programming to be "nice" all the time, even when people are violating your boundaries.

## $\mathcal{T}$IME BANDITS

THE FIRST kind of boundary violators, *time bandits*, literally hold you up when you're on the way to do something else. They're usually lonely, frustrated individuals looking for attention.

Tina is a bank supervisor with two time bandits in her office—Joanne and Myra. The first thing in the morning, Joanne ambushes Tina in the outer office to tell her about embarrassing personal problems—her latest yeast infection or colitis attack. At the end of the day, when Tina tries to wrap things up, in comes Myra to complain about some problem she's having—with the staff, the computers, or the furniture in her office.

Whether they ambush you with trivial conversation, complaints, or personal problems, time bandits can hold you up, waste your time, and throw you off track.

### TAKING POSITIVE ACTION

Think of the last time you encountered a time bandit. Since such people literally steal your time, see this person in a Wild West costume—black cowboy hat, six-shooters, and a red bandanna, saying, "This is a stickup."

The next time someone tries to hold you up, smile and remember the image:

- See him or her in the time bandit costume.
- Don't react. Don't be drawn into the time bandit's trap. Define your territory with verbal cues: "What can I do for you? I only have five minutes" or "I can't talk now. Can we set up a time to meet later?" But say this only if you really want to talk to the person later.
- If you need something from the person, define your territory and get to the point: "I'd like to talk to you about this week's sales report. Do you have ten minutes?"
- If the person who interrupts you is a friend with a real problem and it's not an emergency, schedule a time to talk about it later. Try to move your friend from complaint to positive action by asking, "What would you like to have happen?" and "What are you going to do about it?"

## SPACE INVADERS

SPACE INVADERS sounds like science fiction—alien beings dropping in on you from another world. They are uninvited guests who invade your territory when you're trying to do something else—concentrate, relax, complete a project, finish your dinner—you name it. Space invaders are no respecters of privacy.

They come in different forms, beaming themselves in on you either electronically or in person. Julie is a freelance writer who does much of her work at home, writing celebrity biographies. Her neighbors are always ringing her doorbell and dropping by to chat, intrigued by the glamour and gossip of Julie's life. Looking for diversion, they do not respect her privacy. These people are space invaders. Other, more lovable space invaders are Julie's husband and children, who come into her home office when she's working, interrupting her with questions, conversation, and pleas for attention. Or the children want to play with her computer. While she loves them, she'd rather not be interrupted when she's working on deadline projects.

## TAKING POSITIVE ACTION

Think of the last time someone invaded your space. Visualize this person in a fluorescent green space suit emerging from a flying saucer with a ray gun ready to zap you. Smile as you make the image as outrageous as possible. After all, this person is a space invader.

The next time someone invades your space, whether at home or at work:

- Visualize this person in the space invader costume.
- Don't react. Don't let the space invader stun you into submission or drag you off into another dimension.
- Define your space with visual and verbal cues. Julie has been putting a DO NOT DISTURB sign on her door and reminding her children, "Mommy's busy now," when she's in the middle of an important project. (She also lets her family know when she *will* be available for them.) When neighbors come by to chat, she either doesn't answer the door or tells them, "This isn't a good time," and arranges to see them later.

Prevent future invasions in your life by developing strategies for defining your space, using clear and consistent communication.

- If you don't take business calls at home, tell your co-workers and get a machine to screen your calls.
- If someone drops by when you're busy, tell the person so and set up an appointment for later.
- If a space invader ignores your verbal cues, you may need to be more direct. The next time he or she drops by, don't answer the door.
- If you have children, they will respect your boundaries if you give clear signals for when "Mommy's busy" and reinforce them consistently. But also make sure your children get the care they need and know when you *will* be available to them.
- If you're working on a deadline, discourage space invaders by asking your secretary to screen calls, closing your door, or posting a sign that you're "in conference" and will be available at a designated time.

## $\mathcal{M}$ANAGING ELECTRONIC INVADERS: THE PHONE AND E-MAIL

SPACE INVADERS come in nonhuman forms as well. The phone is the most outrageous space invader. Its insistent ringing interrupts people when they're at work, asleep, in the shower, or in the middle of dinner. Personally, I would not want to interrupt any of my friends so rudely. Don't let the phone tyrannize over your life.

Here are some ways to keep the phone from making your life unmanageable:

- Get a recorder to answer your calls, then return them all at a convenient time. Many people return calls at the end of the day or during a break between projects. This also works for E-mail. Don't answer every message when it comes in, or your days will be fractured by interruptions. E-mail and voice mail have brought a chronic sense of urgency to many offices, but they're really just notes from other people, conveyed electronically. Don't let them become space invaders.

- Define your space on the phone the same way you do in person. Tell the other person how much time you have and the purpose of the call. Respect the other person's time boundaries as well. Ask, "Do you have ten minutes to talk about _____?"

- If you're returning a call, ask the person the purpose of the call. Get right to the point.

- Sometimes people call when they just want to visit. If you don't mind spending an hour or so on the phone with them, fine. If not, don't let them catch you off guard. Tell the other person, "I don't have time to visit right now." Arrange to get together for lunch or coffee when you have the time.

## $\mathcal{G}$OOD EXIT LINES

WITH SPACE invaders, you'll often need a good exit line to help you get on with your life. I've heard lots of ingenious exit lines. Some women get off the phone by saying, "I have to check something in the kitchen." I used to rely on my dog as an excuse—saying I had to get off the phone to let my dog out.

But kitchens and dogs can take us only so far. The best exit line is short, precise, and unapologetic. "I have to go now" and "I have another appointment" need no further explanation.

Some boundary violators will ignore your exit line. After all, these people don't *want* to stop talking. You do. Repeat your exit line and say good-bye. Then take action. Leave—hang up the phone or start walking.

People may get upset when you set boundaries because you're not giving them what they want. It takes courage and discipline to break old habits of being "nice" all the time in order to live your own life.

If someone doesn't respect your boundaries, you have an imbalanced relationship. Getting back in balance will require some adjustments. Listen to the other person with compassion, but set your boundaries and honor them. You can't expect other people to respect your boundaries unless you show them the way. Gradually, your interactions will change. Some relationships will adjust while others will not endure. But in time, the people in your life will respect your boundaries and you'll have more power and peace of mind.

## *P*ERSONAL RESPONSIBILITY AND BALANCE

LIVING RESPONSIBLY means striking a healthy balance between your relationships to others and to yourself. Maintaining this balance often requires the discipline of a samurai.

At times the rush of demands in our lives can feel like a tidal wave. We must be mindful or these powerful currents will knock us down and drag us into their wake. Instead of resenting the struggle, we can see it as an opportunity to develop valuable skills.

As weight training uses resistance to develop our muscles, we can use life's daily demands as resistance to develop our inner strength. In a powerful personal exercise no one around us will even notice, we can gently but firmly decline invitations to waste our time, delegate whenever possible, and resist external demands in order to be true to ourselves. Here are some helpful guidelines:

- *Stop subordinating yourself to your work.* Can you leave work on your desk at the end of the day or do you "need" to finish every project before leaving? If you feel you have to finish everything, stop subordinating yourself. Do your best and when it's time to leave, write a note to yourself about where to pick up tomorrow. Keep a pack of Post-its for this purpose. Tomorrow you'll return with fresh insights. Your work will improve, and so will your quality of life.
- *Don't let work or family responsibilities spill into your time for regular exercise, rest, and renewal.* Obviously, if someone breaks a leg, you won't let your evening workout keep you from driving her to the hospital. But don't habitually neglect your own needs to handle interruptions and last-minute requests. Schedule a regular time to do the things you need. Resist last-minute interruptions unless they're really emergencies. Tell people, "I have an appointment." You do—with yourself. Keep your commitments to yourself as sacred as those you make to others.

Redefining responsibility means not subordinating your inner life to external demands. You can delegate many tasks at home and work but your workouts and your spiritual growth are not among them. Only *you* can be responsible to yourself, to your own values and needs, as well as to those you love. Remember to practice the power of simplicity, giving yourself room to grow and flourish.

■ *Practice everyday* misogi *by creating your own maintenance cycle.*

The wisdom of Tao tells us that in nature, there's a season for everything, a time to plant and a time to harvest. You can simplify household maintenance with the momentum of recurrent cycles. Fill in the blanks, setting up a pattern that works best for you (laundry on Monday, grocery shopping on Tuesday, and so on) and your chores will get done in their own natural rhythm.

| DAY OF THE WEEK | REGULAR MAINTENANCE |
|-----------------|---------------------|
| Monday | _____ |
| Tuesday | _____ |
| Wednesday | _____ |
| Thursday | _____ |
| Friday | _____ |
| Saturday | _____ |
| Sunday | _____ |

■ *Simplify daily life with effective strategies.*

Women with families often find themselves overwhelmed with responsibilities. If this includes you, you're probably doing more than your share. Claim greater power and peace by:

- *Eliminating the nonessentials.* Clearing away clutter on table-tops makes them easier to keep clean. What can you put away so it doesn't just sit there and collect dust?

- *Alternating chores.* Each week do a surface cleaning in most rooms, a more thorough job in the bathroom this week, the kitchen or another room the next.

- *Asking your family to participate more.* Include *everyone* in the system. Even very young children can pick up their clothes and put their toys away—learning responsibility in the process. They can also do simple chores. My little brother began helping out at age five, emptying all the trash on Saturday while the rest of us cleaned house.

- *Creating a rhythm that works for you.* One couple I know takes turns making dinner so that one person is "on duty" while the other person has that time free—every other night. They share other chores as well.

- *Using your ingenuity.* My friend Cyndi turned household chores into a game that both she and her husband can win. She put a list of all their weekly chores on the refrigerator. Each week, whenever Cyndi and Mike do some of the chores, they check off the task and write their initials beside it. At the end of the week, the one with the most checks chooses the movie or restaurant they go to that weekend.

- *Delegating effectively.* If you and your family are too busy to take care of the yard, hire a local teenager to do it for you.

- *Building cooperative arrangements.* If you have children, perhaps an older neighbor would trade child care for a weekly trip to the store. Make a cooperative arrangement with other nearby mothers to share child care and driving, leaving you all with more time and building a stronger sense of community in the process.

If you're feeling overwhelmed, start simplifying your life by looking beyond the details. By thinking in larger systems, you'll come up with solutions that include your family, friends, and community, making *all* of your lives work better.

■ *Simplifying practices to remember:*

- Create regular margins in your life, drawing upon the power of *yohaku.*
- Clear away clutter from your home and your life with ongoing *misogi.*
- Honor your own boundaries, practicing the art of *budo.*

# The Lesson of Natural Cycles

Ten thousand things move around you.
In detachment, perceive the cycles.
Watch each return to the source.
Returning to the source is harmony
With the way of nature.
Knowing the cycles brings wisdom.
Not knowing brings confusion.

*TAO, 16* [1]

aking leaves one crisp autumn day put me in touch with the lesson of cycles and seasons. The fallen leaves were scattered on the grass in mosaic patterns of red, green, and gold. Some leaves were yellow tipped with red, like fire. Others were solid red or butter yellow, so perfect I wanted to pick them up and take them inside. As I raked, more leaves circled down from the trees. They were maple leaves, five-pointed, like bright stars falling to earth.

I raked the colorful leaves into compost piles at the side of the yard, where they would turn rusty brown, be broken down by the elements, and return to earth to nourish a new burst of life in the spring. The bright profusion of green leaves would, in turn, be transformed into another shower of red and gold next fall. Like a familiar refrain in the symphony of nature, the days and weeks go by, the seasons come round again, and the cycle continues.

It is written in *Ecclesiastes,* "To every thing there is a season and a time to every purpose under heaven." We each have our daily cycles, circadian rhythms, in which our energy ebbs and flows with predictable regularity. Some of us are morning people, beginning the day with a rush of active *yang* energy. Others are more *yin,* more contemplative in the morning, working up to a season of *yang* as the day moves on. Some people are more animated at night while others withdraw at sundown into the quieter rhythms of *yin.*

## *R*ECOGNIZING YOUR DAILY CYCLES

You can bring greater power into your life by honoring your daily cycles, discovering your own highs and lows and using them to advantage. Chart your own circadian rhythms by marking the number from 1 (low) to 5 (high) that describes your energy level at different times of the day:

- When I wake up in the morning I feel: groggy—
  1 2 3 4 5—awake and ready to go.
- At 10:00 A.M. I feel: tired—1 2 3 4 5—focused and energetic.

- At noon I feel: my energies waning—1 2 3 4 5—energetic.
- After lunch I feel: my energies lag—1 2 3 4 5—invigorated.
- At 3:00 P.M. I feel: sluggish and sleepy—1 2 3 4 5—energetic.
- At 5:00 P.M. I feel: tired—1 2 3 4 5—energetic.
- From 7:00 to 9:00 P.M. I feel: like winding down—1 2 3 4 5—a second wind.
- At 10:00 P.M. I am: ready for bed—1 2 3 4 5—energetic: the night is young.
- At _____ o'clock, my energies are low and I feel like going to sleep.

The last question marks the end of your circadian cycle. The rest will give you important insights into the ebb and flow of your daily energies. The higher numbers, the 4's and 5's, are your peak energy periods. The 1's and 2's are your lows. Most of us have a period of high energy in the morning followed by a dip in our energies in midafternoon, then another period of rising energy that gradually wanes, preparing us for sleep.

## USING YOUR PRIME TIME

YOUR MOST energetic period is your "prime time," when you are most focused and productive. Ideally, this should be when you do the important things, relegating routine chores to your low energy periods. But most people don't do this. They go through the mail when they arrive at work, squandering their peak energy hours on mindless tasks and interruptions, beginning the important work as their energy starts to fade. Years ago, a wise physicist shared with me his secret of using circadian rhythms to advantage. He scheduled his research during his prime time, his teaching during his second burst of energy, and saved routine chores like opening the mail and returning calls for 3:00 in the afternoon, when, he said, he could never do anything productive anyway.

### Working with the Cycles

As much as possible, structure your day around your own energy highs and lows. Use your most creative time to advantage.

- If you work in an office, hold your calls and close your door during your prime time, using this period for focused concentration, long-range planning, and important projects.
- If you work at home, do important tasks when your energy is highest. Then return calls, open your mail, and run errands during your lag time. Find your own personal balance between your work and homelife.
- A brisk walk or a good workout near the end of the day will give you another round of clarity and renewed energy. Use this time to advantage as well, not just for work but to celebrate life.

Many people get so caught up in work they neglect their lives. Some couples come and go like sleepwalkers, their ardor dimmed by dull routine. Each morning they gulp their coffee and dash off in different directions. They come to life at work, then return home in hollow-eyed exhaustion to share the dregs of the day with each other. Relationships are living things with their own energy cycles that need culti-

vation. Remember to spend some of your prime time with
the ones you love.

## ℋonoring the Cycles Within and Around You

LIVING WITH greater power and peace means becoming
more mindful of the cycles within and around you. This does
*not* mean being dominated or driven by them. Nor does it
mean denying them. Wise women recognize the cycles and
work *with* them to create new forms of harmony.

The moon waxes and wanes in monthly cycles, influenc-
ing the tides, women's periods,[2] the growing phases of
plants, and other subtle energies in our world. For centuries
farmers have planted their seeds during the new moon when
they germinate more rapidly.

By becoming more mindful of your own monthly cycles,
you can use these times to advantage. Working *with* the natural process of your menstrual cycle instead of fighting or
ignoring it can even reduce or eliminate cramps, according
to holistic gynecologist Dr. Christiane Northrup.

- Next month, don't run yourself down with frantic *yang*
  activity when your body is in a natural *yin* phase.
- Slow down for a couple of days and give yourself margins to do whatever relaxes and renews you—soaking
  in a warm bath, curling up with a heating pad, or taking
  a leisurely walk.
- Listen to your self: your body, your mind, and your
  own intuitive wisdom which is stronger for many
  women during their periods.

Taking this time each month to honor the cycle of life within
you will put you in touch with yourself on a deeper level.[3]

# THE SEASONS OF OUR LIVES

EACH LIFE has its own cycles: times of initiation, growth, fruition, and contemplation. Developmental psychologists have described the chronological seasons: the reckless vitality of youth when we dare to reach out in pursuit of our dreams; the full lives of adulthood when many of those dreams become realities, bringing more complications than we could imagine; the bittersweet season of middle adulthood when we pause to take stock, experiencing both harvest and loss. Finally, there is winter, the season of late adulthood with its own deep lessons of identity and meaning.[4]

Yet, beyond chronology, each life has its own cycles of growth, challenge, and renewal. We all march to different rhythms, ripening at our own pace. Measuring ourselves by others' standards is both unnatural and unwise. Some women are early bloomers, coming into their own in a sunny adolescence while others, still lost in the fog, take much longer. In the natural world, each living thing has its own cycle, each flower its own season—the daffodils and lilacs of early spring, the roses of summer, the chrysanthemums of autumn.

# TO EVERY ENDEAVOR THERE IS A SEASON

THE SEASONS of life repeat themselves with each new relationship or project. Each experience has its own seasons of springtime, summer, fall, and winter. Some are annuals, a new job or relationship that begins with a burst of energy, then fades after one short season. Wisdom is recognizing the end of a cycle, not fighting the inevitable but knowing when to move on.

As the new human relations director for a large computer firm, Shelly began her job with boundless enthusiasm. She developed a new benefits package for employees, setting up seminars on financial planning. She was accessible and up-beat, developing an enthusiastic following among the employees and winning high evaluations from her supervisor.

Then her supervisor retired, and a new man was hired whose personality clashed dramatically with hers. He discounted her suggestions, cut her budget, and criticized her management style. The irresistible force of Shelly's momentum was blocked by the immovable object supervising her. She tried working with him, working around him, wearing down his resistance, and enlisting the support of others, but nothing worked. She could go no further in this job without compromising herself. The only healthy option was to start sending out her résumé. She had hit the ceiling in her current position.

While some endeavors last only one short season, others are perennial, returning again for many new springtimes, renewing us as they renew themselves. Wisdom involves recognition and cultivation.

The marriage of one couple I know has flourished for many cycles. Michael and Marilyn married after high school graduation, raised three children, coped with tight budgets, the competing demands of graduate school, building a career in scientific research, and caring for their growing family. Together they dealt with the challenge of serious illness and his parents' passing. As their last child leaves home and they welcome their first grandchild, they have found, in the autumn of middle adulthood, another season of renewal, loving and appreciating each other on a deeper level. At this stage of life's journey, they work together on their research and walk together hand in hand, blending the richness of autumn with the romance of second spring.[5]

## $\mathcal{C}$ULTIVATING CYCLES OF RENEWAL

EVERY LONG-TERM relationship or career needs *cultivation* to create new seasons of discovery and renewal.

- If you've been coasting in your job, taking it for granted, don't wait until your energies go stale. Learn a new skill. Take on a new project. Get involved in your professional organization.
- In your relationship, explore ways to renew your sense of intimacy and adventure. Don't just do chores together. Find ways to break away from routine. Share something you both believe in. Build houses together for Habitat for Humanity. Play tennis. Learn and laugh and play together regularly. Plan a brief vacation or pack a picnic next weekend and go exploring. Visit an art gallery in the city or search for treasures in second-hand stores. Take a hike in the woods or a walk on the pier. Renew your relationship with a new sense of discovery.

## $\mathcal{T}$HE LESSON OF SPRINGTIME: A TIME TO BEGIN

YOU CAN bring more power and peace to your life by recognizing the four seasons in every experience and following their lessons. New projects or relationships are filled with the energies of spring. New beginnings always make us feel young again, with what the Buddhists call "beginner's mind," the wonder, anxiety, and power that come when we reach out for new possibilities.

New beginnings put you in touch with your innate creative capacity. Beginning something new can fill you with youthful vitality, but it can also lead to youthful impetuousness. The excitement of newness often keeps people from thinking things through. They leap into commitments with romantic abandon, whether the experience is a relationship, an expensive purchase, or a career move.

Holly is always starting new projects, falling for new men. Her life is one long adventure but she never seems to get beyond beginnings. Her closets are full of impulsive purchases and her guest room is filled with unfinished projects—cans of herbal supplements she'd agreed to sell, a knitting machine and skeins of yarn from another venture. She signed up for a computer class but dropped out to take a Mediterranean cruise for the holidays, hoping, this time, to meet the perfect man. Holly zigzags through life, jumping from one impulse to another, convinced there's always something more on the horizon.

The *gift* of new beginnings is their power to renew you, to add zest to your life. The *lesson* of beginnings is discernment. Remember to look beyond your initial enthusiasm long enough to ask whether this new beginning is really right for you.

At the next new beginning, stop and ask yourself:

"What am I beginning and why?"
"Does this choice make sense in my life now?"

## *T*HE LESSON OF SUMMER: A TIME TO CULTIVATE

THE SEASON of summer brings different challenges. New projects take time to grow. They need cultivation. The *les-*

*son* here is patience. We need to persevere and trust the process.

Louise begins diets and exercise programs with great enthusiasm, then gives up before she sees any results. She's been on the grapefruit diet, the Fit for Life diet, the macrobiotic diet, and the live foods diet. She has a Nordic track in her living room and a mountain bike in her garage, both nearly new. She joined a gym, bought new exercise clothes, then lost interest after a few weeks.

If you're like Louise and become impatient before you see results, you're not alone. It takes time to establish new habits, just as it takes time for the vegetables I plant each spring to grow and ripen. The key is to persevere while you cultivate your garden—or your new project. Research has shown that it takes at least thirty days to make any new behavior a part of your life. If you can persevere for thirty days, you'll build an inner momentum that will move you toward your goal.

Remember the wisdom of summer: Be patient with the process. The *gift* of summer is the strength of character that comes from setting goals and moving toward completion. This daily discipline gives us greater self-respect and personal power, perhaps even more important in the long run than the goal we're seeking.

If you find yourself losing heart in what seems a long growing season, remember:

- *To keep building momentum,* following the thirty-day rule.
- *To cultivate this new behavior.* If you're on a diet, avoid temptations like the doughnut shop near work. Cultivate healthy alternatives. When you leave for work, take some fresh fruit or a bagel with fat-free cream cheese in your briefcase so you won't be tempted.

- *To reward yourself for progress.* Have you stayed on your diet for a week? Then treat yourself to a movie or something else you'll enjoy. Set a new reward for next week. Each day, congratulate yourself on your progress.

## THE LESSON OF AUTUMN: A TIME TO HARVEST

AUTUMN BRINGS the season of harvest, a time to gather in the fruits of our labors. The *lesson* here is timing. Some of us are excited by the prospect of completion. Impatient, we rush to finish our projects too soon, picking our fruit before it's ripe. I've always been excited by what psychologists call the "goal gradient effect." I'll rush to complete a project, sometimes skipping an essential detail.

Other people can't bear to end a project. They miss the time of harvest because of insecurity, letting the fruit stay on the vine until it rots. Loretta won't finish a report until she's convinced everything is perfect, so she misses one deadline after another, creating bottlenecks at work, causing paperwork to pile up, and irritating her supervisor and coworkers. She refuses to delegate to her staff, handling every detail to be sure it's right. Her life is an endless pile of paperwork, her nights short on sleep, her days filled with guilt and frustration.

Autumn is the season of harvest, both within and around us. One of its *gifts* is always greater insight into ourselves as we become more mindful of how we handle endings. When approaching the end of a project, ask yourself:

"Am I finished? Is the time ripe for harvest?"
"How do I know?"

If you're in doubt, step back and consider the evidence. Ask someone you trust for advice. If the time is right, then take action. Complete the job. If you still find it hard to take action, get help. Team up with someone you trust to increase your effectiveness and expand your knowledge base. Watch how this person handles endings. Or sign up for a course in time management. Awareness is power. As you learn to balance your natural tendencies, you'll be able to complete your projects with precision and grace.

## $C$HE LESSON OF WINTER: A TIME TO REFLECT

THE SEASON of winter offers us a chance to slow down and reflect on what we've learned. But many people never do this. At the end of any experience, some women experience the equivalent of postpartum depression. Something that has filled their lives with significance is suddenly gone. They rush to fill the emptiness.

After her divorce from Jack, Brenda was almost never home. She took on new responsibilities at work, exercised five nights a week, took a music class at the local community college, and signed up as volunteer coordinator at her church. With the demands of her job, workouts, classes, and church, there was no time for her to feel the loss in her personal life, let alone learn from it.

Like Brenda, many of us don't feel right unless we're constantly in motion. Pushed along by our noisy, busy culture, we are in such a hurry at the end of something that we rush to fill the gap with something else. We often skip the subtle season of reflection and the wisdom it offers.

Following the Tao of womanhood means taking time to reflect, even if it involves working through feelings of loss, disappointment, and pain. We reject the temptation to rush into another round of activity that would only numb us to our inner life. Becoming more mindful during our seasons of winter, reflecting upon our feelings, our dreams, and the patterns of our lives, will help us make wiser choices in the future.

At the end of an experience, remember to ask yourself:

"What did I learn from the process?"
"How can I apply this lesson next time?"

Write down your answers and keep them to review when you begin another similar experience.

## SEASONS OF CHALLENGE AND CHANGE

EACH LIFE has its own seasons of challenge and change. From hopeful beginnings, our relationships and careers can grow, prosper, and then go to seed. Recognizing these seasons and keeping our eyes open to new possibilities can bring our lives greater meaning and power.

As the autumn leaves fall from the trees, a season of change forces us to let go of old patterns and begin anew. Instead of resenting and resisting change, we can seize this opportunity to give our lives greater direction.

A few years ago, Frances found herself in such a season. The familiar structure of her life had worn away. After a long marriage, her divorce settlement left her with a division of property, decades of memories, and her own life to reinvent.

She had her materials—her writing, her poet's eye for beauty, the memories of her childhood home in Georgia, and a longing to make a new home for herself. In time she began a new relationship with another writer.

After a busy year of teaching at universities in the Bay Area, she and Ed spent a summer in Italy. Leaving behind the hectic pace of their professional lives, they explored the age-old culture. Enjoying the warmth of the Mediterranean sun and the flavor of life in Italy, Frances dreamed of finding a home there, a place for new beginnings, seven thousand miles from anything she'd ever known.

They looked at houses, weighing their price in millions of lire against their teachers' salaries. Then one day she took a deep breath and sank her life savings into an abandoned farmhouse in Tuscany. The house in the hills outside Cortona had been neglected for thirty years. Its gardens were overgrown with weeds, its floors covered with layers of dust. But the house held a promise, the view was magnificent, and they celebrated their outrageous purchase with glasses of prosecco and dinner under the stars.

During the long summers and the Christmas holidays, she and Ed slowly brought the old house back to life. By necessity and by choice, they did much of the work themselves, cutting back the weeds, painting the walls, refinishing and sealing the dark wooden beams and waxing the old floors until they shone. From an abandoned shell, the house became a home, its beauty rising to console them after a long day's work.

Their lives deliberately simplified by the work of restoration, they arose early each morning, filled with the energy of new beginnings. Beyond the hard work was the joy of seeing their work take shape. Returning to their home in Italy each summer and during school vacations, they found themselves in a different world where they could celebrate life, enjoy fruit from their own orchard, and savor the classic cuisine of Tuscany. In the refuge of their new home, they found time to read, reflect, and write.

Restoring the house was as much an inner as an outer process. Each year, the seasons took on added significance, developing their own rhythm as they spent the busy academic year in the Bay Area and summers in Italy. The house was called Bramasole, which means in Italian "a yearning for the sun,"[6] and, even in memory, the Italian sun gave a new warmth to their lives. Frances and Ed brought back Italian clothes, classic recipes, and a cappuccino machine to their house in San Francisco, gentle reminders to enjoy *la dolce vita*, the sweetness of life, in the midst of their busy schedules. At the end of the term, they went home to Bramasole to have their senses restored by life on an Italian hillside, under a broad expanse of sky, thousands of miles from all the stress they'd left behind.

As the years circled by, the house grew more beautiful and their relationship stronger with this shared re-creation and celebration of life. After six years, Frances paused to reflect about her creative response to a season of change. When divorce shattered her old life, she had reached out to create a new one. "I wanted to change my life, and that's one of the reasons I did this," she said. "When change is going to happen to you, if you don't do something that moves you forward in your thinking, then you find yourself repeating what you know. I'd come to a point when I felt I wanted to do something I did *not* know how to do"[7] Embraced in this way, a season of change offers each of us a chance to renew and redefine our lives.

With their house in the sun, she and her new love created a fresh life for themselves, a life that recalls the country charm of her Georgia childhood, while offering them both a new world to explore.

### €MBRACING CHANGE CREATIVELY

IF YOU find yourself in a season of challenge and change, then it's time to decide what to keep, what to release, what seeds to save for another spring. First ask yourself some questions.

- What old patterns do I want to release from my life?
- What have I been missing? What do I need more of?
- Is there a dream I've been wanting to realize? All of us have unfulfilled longings, childhood dreams. If your life is undergoing major change, this may be the time to get back in touch with your dreams.
- What do I need to make my dream a reality? Do you need to do some journaling, some inner work before launching out into external change?

After answering these questions, you'll need to do some exploring. Frances looked at many houses before choosing the right one. If you're considering buying a house, changing careers, or another new adventure, now's the time to:

- Get more information. This might mean getting catalogs and brochures, looking at listings, consulting reference materials at your local library.
- Talk to people who've done something like this before.
- Brainstorm with a friend, listing all the pluses and minuses you can think of.
- Visualize yourself doing this. How does it feel?

When you've done enough exploring, examining some options, discarding others, you're ready to chart a new path to your future.

- Make yourself a plan. Where do you want to go? What do you need to get there? Write down a list of steps in logical sequence.

- Try to anticipate any hazards, asking what might go wrong and coming up with possible solutions. Even then, you cannot anticipate them all. Every new adventure is a risk. Exploring the unknown, you will meet unforeseen challenges. You will have to face your fears of failure and rejection at several points along the way. But the journey will make you strong, building your trust in yourself and your faith in life.
- Take that first step, mindful of where it leads and how you feel about it.
- Then stop to reflect. Were there any surprises? Do you need to make any adjustments in your plan? Take the necessary action. If you're unsure of what to do next, get more information.
- When you're ready for the next step, take it, and ask yourself the same questions.

A process of mindful change is an ongoing discovery. One step leads to the next, revealing where to go and what to do. The *Tao Te Ching* tells us: "A journey of a thousand miles begins with a single step" (*Tao*, 64). When we have the courage to take that step, we begin our own creative adventure.

A season of change can be a time of harvest, replete with possibility for those who have eyes to see. Knowing what to keep and what to let go, having the courage to begin again, can help you, too, make a new home for yourself and build the life of your dreams.

力 *Pointers for Greater Power and Peace*

*Here are some reminders about honoring the cycles in your life.*

■ **Remember to work in harmony with the cycles.**

- Be mindful of your own circadian rhythms when planning your daily activities.
- Take time each month to slow down and get back in touch with your intuition.
- Become more aware of the cycles around you, noting the energy highs and lows of other people and activities in your life so that you can make wiser choices.

■ *Recognize that each relationship, career, or project has its own life cycle.*

Remember the wisdom of each season, being more mindful of beginnings, middles, and endings, as well as the need to reflect when a cycle is completed.

## PART II

The Yang of
Personal Power

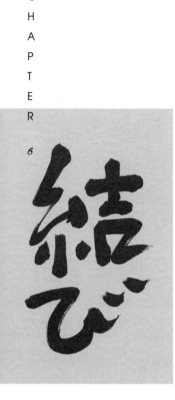

# The Lesson of Timing

Women of Tao
Live close to nature.
Their actions flow from the heart.
In words, they are true,
In decisions, just,
In their choices,
Aware of the timing.

*T A O , 8* [1]

*W*hen I was ten, my family lived in the Philippine Islands. We had a house with windows made of seashells. Mango and papaya trees grew in our yard, and our neighborhood was a close-knit group of families. My best friend, Missy Connor, the only other girl my age, lived in the house across the street.

On quiet tropical afternoons, Missy and I would stand watching her grandmother as she sat at her loom, with her white hair piled high on her head, marking time with colorful yarns and rhythmic motion. The loom took up nearly half the space in her bedroom. Its warp strands threaded vertically on large wooden frames reminded me of some primordial harp. Spreading her skeins of yarn in rainbow colors across the bed, she'd plan her next design, then thread the yarn into wooden shuttles that danced across the warp strands in her agile hands.

Back and forth, she moved with a smile, working the foot treadles, shifting the frames as she turned what seemed just rows of string into bright and beautiful cloth. I'd watch in amazement, unable to put into words what I saw. I didn't know it then but weaving is one of the oldest arts, practiced primarily by women, with looms dating back to 4400 B.C. Graceful and methodical as she worked with her loom, my friend's grandmother was like Penelope weaving in the *Odyssey*. She seemed to me archetypal, like the generations of women throughout history who have woven the strands of time into the varied fabric of their lives.

Time is the loom on which each of us practices her own personal artistry. The hours of the day and the other "givens" of our lives are the warp strands, threaded vertically through our days. We respond to them with the bright-colored yarns of our passions, our intentions, our choices, weaving our carefully made plans together with surprise and opportunity, into our own design. As we move through the hours of the day with the yarns of our personal response—the golden strands of joy, the dark yarn of our sorrow—each of us marks the time, retracing our own themes, discovering new variations, creating a pattern unique to ourselves.

In managing our time, awareness brings us power. To be

good weavers, we must be aware of our choices. For mindless action produces messy results—loose threads, haphazard patterns, chaotic lives. Or we weave our patterns reactively, following someone else's design.

Many women today feel their lives coming unraveled because they're not aware of their timing. They rush from one event to the next, too distracted by details to see the pattern they're creating. Caught up in compulsive activity, they find the strands of life's tapestry becoming a tangled mess.

## Becoming More Aware of Your Attitudes

WHEN YOU are aware of your timing, your life reflects your deepest values, tracing the subtle patterns of your dreams. But many of us develop habits that sabotage our timing. Entangled in external demands, we fail to exercise our creative power. If your life feels too hectic, one of these habits may be sabotaging you.

*You can't say no.* Betty's life is a nonstop set of obligations. A busy teacher, community leader, and mother of three, she feels she must take care of everything. Her days are filled with more responsibilities than she can handle.
Look at the tempo of your life.

- Are your days filled with one obligation after another?
- Have you made yourself indispensable to too many people?

If you're being pulled in too many directions, then it's time to cut back, bind off some of those threads. Focus on what's really important. Simplify your design. This chapter will show you how.

*You want to prove you're strong.* A busy attorney specializing in high-level litigation, Donna prides herself on her independence. She feels that women who ask for help are weak, so she does everything herself. She takes the most difficult cases, volunteers for demanding *pro bono* work, even lifts heavy water bottles to fill the cooler when one of her male clerks could do the job.

- Do you do things to "prove" your strength and stamina?
- Are you reluctant to ask for help?

Wearing yourself out trying to prove something demonstrates not your strength but your stubbornness. Simplify your motives and your life. Don't fill up your time with mindless efforts to prove yourself.

*You are unwilling to delegate.* Tina and Jim are both busy insurance executives, but Jim delegates routine work to his secretary, leaving himself time to plan while Tina is stretched to the limit juggling clients, calls, and miscellaneous chores. Men are usually more comfortable delegating routine chores. To use your time more wisely, you, too, need to delegate. Look around you.

- Have you been mindlessly doing routine work when someone else could do it for you?

If you're in more than an entry-level position, doing your own photocopying and other routine work might seem harmless, but it steals your time from the important things, overloading your schedule. As you move forward in life, don't keep doing all the routine work you used to do. To make room for new challenges, delegate as much as possible: to your assistants, your colleagues, your friends, your children. Ask, "Is there someone else who could do this better?" Or "Should someone else be doing this?" Use modern conveniences like computers and answering machines to save time and simplify your life.

*You get distracted because you don't prioritize.* An interior designer with a growing clientele, Liz rushes from one unfinished task to the next, her life a series of frustrations.

- If you've been feeling overwhelmed, remember to review your goals from Chapter 2 and prioritize your plans each day.
- When you forget something important because of too many loose ends in your life, take time to catch your breath. Step back and ask yourself, "What's really important to me now?"

*You subordinate yourself to a job, a project, a relationship.* A political journalist with a heart as wide as the Montana sky, Monica always puts herself last. She postpones routine maintenance to help a friend, volunteer for a good cause, or handle a big project. Without regular maintenance, her car breaks down and her house is a shambles. She comes home after a long day to find that her cupboards are bare, so she makes do with a cup of soup for dinner before tackling another project she's brought home.

Do you forget to weave time for yourself and regular maintenance into your busy days?

- Make a list of all the things you need to do to keep your life together: maintenance for your body, your hair, your teeth, your diet, your house, your car.
- For the next three months, set up appointments to take care of them.
- When you get your teeth cleaned, your hair cut, or the oil changed in your car, mark the time for your next appointment on your calendar.
- Schedule your maintenance activities regularly, *before* making commitments in your work or social life. You can't delegate personal maintenance. If you don't take care of yourself, who will?

*You cut your margins too thin, trying to fit "just one more thing" into an already crammed schedule.* Laura is a technical writer who's always running late because she tries to handle "just one more thing" on her desk before meeting a friend for lunch. Or she stops for just "one more errand" en route to an appointment. She cuts her margins so thin she's under constant time stress. Her chronic lateness upsets other people and makes her feel inadequate because she's always apologizing.

If this pattern sounds familiar, stop cutting your margins so thin.

- If it takes at least thirty minutes to drive to the dentist's office, allow forty-five minutes to an hour.
- Give yourself margins for traffic and other delays.
- If you need the margin, you've got it. If not, you've given yourself time to breathe and collect yourself.
- Bring along a book to read when you find yourself with "extra" time.

\*   \*   \*

THE TIME management lessons in this chapter will help you break free of these counterproductive habits. Learning the skill of *ma-ai*, you'll use pauses to keep from being caught up in reactive patterns. You'll learn to weave your energies together with those of others in the art of *musubi*, avoiding the time stress from overload and procrastination. Finally, you'll learn how to practice *honorable closure*, binding off a project, job, or relationship with mindfulness and integrity.

## THE LESSON OF MA-AI

MA-AI IS a term from aikido that means an interval, the distance in time or space between two actions, two people, two objects.[2] But the concept extends far beyond the martial arts. Everything in the universe has its own optimal *ma-ai*. Plants need water at regular intervals. If you wait too long between waterings, your plants will die from drought. If you water too often, they die from root rot. In the rhythm of nature, each plant has its own needs, its own intervals, its own *ma-ai*.

Music, theater, and dance also demonstrate *ma-ai*. Without alternating intervals of sound and silence there would be no music; the relentless blaring of an instrument would sound like a stuck car horn. The intervals *between* sounds, movements, and gestures are as essential as the actions themselves. The sounds or movements are *yang*, the pauses *yin*, together comprising harmony.

In harmonious relationships, as well, there are intervals, alternating times of togetherness and solitude. Too much togetherness and we feel crowded. Too little, and we drift apart. Each relationship must find its own *ma-ai*, blending the needs of the people involved.

In the timing of our lives, *ma-ai* is the essential interval between action and response that helps us live more effectively. The optimal *ma-ai* depends on the circumstances. It is neither too fast—resulting in hasty, foolhardy action—nor too slow—mindless delay and procrastination.

Using *ma-ai* can keep you from being overloaded and overwhelmed. Instead of rushing into new commitments, use the interval to advantage. Don't respond immediately to every offer or invitation. Take your *ma-ai*, giving yourself time to think about it. Tell the other person, "Let me check my calendar and get back to you." The time this takes will keep you from being reactive. Use the interval to invoke your awareness, to help you see this new opportunity in perspective. Aware of the larger patterns of your life, you'll make wiser choices.

### How to Improve Your Timing with Ma-ai

Don't react to other people's "urgency." Some people purposely *use* urgent approaches to manipulate you. One-day "special" sales often lure people into impulse buying.

Do you buy things you don't need, reacting to aggressive marketing? To prevent impulse buying, I have a personal rule. For any purchase over $100, I come back to buy it the next day. Sometimes I ask the clerk to put it on hold; then I walk out the door. The next day, if I still "need" the item, I'll buy it. If not, or if it's no longer available, I live without it. Either way, I affirm my personal freedom.

Don't react to single events. Look to the larger pattern. The martial arts teach people not to get caught off guard in an attack. Instead of fixating on an opponent's hand or weapon, they look at the whole pattern of energy moving toward them.

Be a martial artist yourself as you respond to each day's

events and opportunities. Don't react to them in isolation but use *ma-ai;* look for the larger patterns. For example:

- If a friend asks, "Are you doing anything Thursday night?" and you see an open space for Thursday evening on your calendar, the reactive answer would be "No," followed up by plans to get together.
- However, if you looked at the *rest* of your calendar and saw a really congested pattern—class on Monday and Wednesday nights, a business meeting Tuesday night, a nonstop day on Thursday, and a big presentation the first thing Friday morning—would you *really* want to spend Thursday night out socializing? It might be your only margin in a hectic week.
- We overschedule ourselves and get run down when we forget to look for the larger patterns. Remember to see things in perspective. Taking the *ma-ai* to respond mindfully helps you look for options. If Thursday is not a good time to see your friend, what about next Tuesday?

## ☯HE LESSON OF *MUSUBI*

THE NEXT lesson in timing, *musubi,* means honoring your own energies while weaving them together with those around you. In the martial arts, *musubi* means unification of opposites, the synergy of two or more energies in a single action. The spiraling action of aikido, which transforms the energies of conflict into cooperation, is one example. An expert skier, one with the mountain as she mindfully darts and dances down the slopes, is another. The dynamic interaction of two Olympic ice skaters, two lovers, two voices combined in song are all *musubi*. Aikido master Mitsugi Saotome says that even "breathing is *musubi*, the resolution of physical and spiritual essence into one, the rhythms of the cycles and relationships of life."[3]

Weaving together the many challenges and demands on your time into meaningful patterns each day is your own practice of *musubi*. Procrastination is bad *musubi*, a mismatch between a person's internal rhythms and external demands. A procrastinator often has low self-esteem and standards so high they paralyze her will. Feeling unequal to a task, she puts it off, unwilling to face it. But the challenge doesn't go away. It usually gets worse.

Shirley is a chronic procrastinator, a writer for a nonprofit agency whose poor *musubi* has undermined her health as well as her career. A perfectionist driven by self-doubt, Shirley made it through college by waiting until the night before a paper was due, using adrenaline anxiety to push through her resistance.

After graduation, she landed a job writing for a consortium of nonprofit agencies in northern California. Her first assignment was a short proposal to the Santa Cruz City Council to save local salmon threatened by industrial pollution. She finished the report in one night and began her new job with a rush of excitement. Her next assignments were studies of the homeless in Santa Cruz County, the murder of baby harp seals, and the relation of nutrition to elementary school performance.

Suddenly, Shirley was overwhelmed. She tried collecting data on the homeless but found the situation too complex. Researching the undernourished children and the baby seals, she looked from one stack of papers to the next, seeing their desperate faces looking up at her. Pushing the papers aside, she went to coffee with a coworker, promising to work on it all tomorrow. The next day came and the next with little progress. Soon Shirley dreaded going to work, coming in late every morning and filling her time with busywork to avoid the challenges on her desk.

She started taking some projects home. But each night she was exhausted just looking at the stacks of paper on her kitchen table. New projects kept coming in and Shirley had to meet with all the different groups. Her days were soon filled with meetings and her meetings filled with apologies.

Weeks went by, and still no progress.To meet the impending deadlines, Shirley resorted to the all-nighters that had gotten her through college, but there was too much to do. She came down with bronchial pneumonia, began missing meetings, calling in sick, asking for extensions, giving one excuse after another, each time feeling worse. Now she sits at home coughing and staring at the stacks of unfinished work, worried about losing her job.

### PREVENTING PROCRASTINATION

Shirley is an extreme, but if you don't catch a procrastination habit in time, it can cause a major portion of your life to come unraveled. Here are some ways to manage your time with the art of *musubi*.

*Use momentum to advantage.* A law of physics tells us that "a body in motion tends to remain in motion. A body at rest tends to remain at rest." Following this principle, Shirley could begin work on a new project right after meeting with the group involved, making notes to herself, setting up a file, and making a preliminary outline while the ideas are still fresh in her mind.

Turn momentum into action to help you get started on a

challenging project or finish a short one while you're still thinking about it.

- Get started on a new project now, even if it only means setting up a file and making preliminary notes. Once you've gotten started, the momentum will carry you through, bringing new ideas and actions.
- Do the minutes right after a meeting, while the ideas are still fresh in your mind.
- Write thank-you notes soon after you've received the gift, while you're still thinking about it.
- Handle correspondence the same way. Answer letters with follow-up notes or phone calls. Don't let piles of correspondence make you feel guilty.

*Turn worry into action.* Worry wastes your time. Don't just worry, do something. If Shirley had spent as much time working on her proposals as she did worrying about them, they would have been done a long time ago. The next time you're worried about a big project, turn worry into positive action. Sit down and make a list of all the things you need to do, then do the first thing on the list. You may not finish the job in one sitting, but just beginning will create a positive momentum.

*Be strategic and get started.* Become your own success coach, breaking a difficult task into smaller parts. Do one part, then reward yourself. Then do the next, followed by another reward.

*Find a system that works for you.* If you have trouble doing routine work like paying your bills on time, create a system. If you get paid twice a month, pay bills twice a month as well. When the bills come in, put them in a pile to pay the next time you get your paycheck. Or if you have one large expense like rent or a house payment, pay that out of one paycheck, and the other bills out of the next. The point is to find a system that works and stick with it.

Shirley could handle her proposals by setting aside one evening a week to check up on pending projects, deciding what actions to take next, and scheduling them on her calendar. She could also build in a reward for herself after each evening session. But the best reward would be staying on track and keeping her life in balance.

*Use different speeds for different projects.* Sometimes it's best to do a task all at once in what time management expert Eugene Griessman calls the "surge mode,"[4] clearing the decks and attacking a project with total concentration. Other times, it's more effective to use the installment plan, plugging along one stage at a time until the work is done. Short-term projects often respond best to the "surge mode," while larger projects require a longer period of sustained effort. One of Shirley's problems was not knowing the difference.

The key here is greater awareness, balancing your response to external demands and opportunities with your own inner rhythms, weaving your own personal pattern of success. With practice you'll use timing to advantage, excelling in the art of *musubi.*

## THE LESSON OF HONORABLE CLOSURE

THE FINAL lesson in time management is honorable closure, binding off the threads when you've completed a pattern in your life[5]. Many of us pride ourselves on persistence. We don't want to be quitters, so we stay involved with unwanted commitments, dead-end jobs, or unhealthy relationships instead of moving on.

Weaving the patterns of our lives, we go through many changes, moving from childhood through the many stages of adulthood. Managing our time wisely means clearing away old patterns to make room for new beginnings. If you don't do this, you'll experience chronic time stress, pulled in too many directions by competing demands. Time management expert Eugene Griessman says, "Don't feel you have to keep doing something that no longer means anything to you."[6] At such times, the most honest thing to do is let go. The art of honorable closure involves knowing when and how to do this.

### A TIME TO LET GO

The wisdom of Ecclesiastes tells us that there is "a time to get, and a time to lose; a time to keep, and a time to cast away." It is time to let go when a job, relationship, or another experience has run its course. Lisa left her job as a spiritual counselor because of mounting frustrations with the "church politics" that overshadowed her efforts and clouded her peace of mind. She made an appointment with the minister, thanked him for what she'd learned, and told him she was leaving to set up an independent practice and pursue her own ministerial studies.

Griessman advises, "When you are reasonably sure you cannot win, no matter how hard you try, make your exit. Don't exhaust your resources in a dishonest game."[7] In a job or relationship, honorable closure is knowing when to cut your losses.

Janet was a young widow who began a relationship with

Gary, a struggling artist. What began as a friendship at church turned into a romance complicated by Gary's neediness and Janet's generosity. Janet loaned him money for art supplies, bought some of his paintings, and referred him to her friends. While she went to work each day at the real estate office, Gary stopped working as a handyman, spending his time visiting art supply stores and setting up a studio in Janet's garage. He became possessive and jealous, calling her at work, insisting on moving in with her, and demanding more money. Realizing she was being used, Janet knew she had to cut her losses and break up with Gary.

### Letting Go

The art of honorable closure involves knowing not only *when* but *how* to let go. It requires honesty with yourself and others and a formal release, a binding off of the old before beginning the new.

Years ago, when I was in graduate school, I fell in love with Tom, a young photographer. But then we entered another phase of life. I got a tenure-track teaching job that required me to spend weeknights preparing classes and doing research. Tom began working as an industrial photographer with a nine-to-five job. After five, he wanted to relax while I needed to work. Wrapped up in my research on a Tuesday night, the most I wanted was a phone call or a short study break, while he wanted to spend the evening together. He offered to make dinner. He brought me presents. He knocked at my door in pain and frustration, while in another kind of frustration I knew I had to do my research or I'd lose my job. We broke up, got back together, broke up, got together again. Finally both of us realized that as much as we cared for each other, our needs were not going to change.

In a bittersweet parting, we thanked each other, cried, even gave each other "going away presents," knowing that in some part of our hearts we'd always care about each other, even though we could go no further together. In all the relationships of my life, that was the most honorable closure.

## PRACTICING HONORABLE CLOSURE

HAVE YOU come to the end of a job, a project, or relationship? Is there something that is not working in your life? These steps can help you create your own honorable closure.

- *Sit down and honestly answer these questions:* What isn't working? How would I like it to be? What do I need to do? Go off by yourself where you won't be disturbed and take time to think.

- *As honestly as possible, communicate your needs to the other person(s).* When Lisa left her position as spiritual counselor, she made an appointment to talk with the minister. When Janet broke off her relationship she told Gary she "could not afford" to give him any more money. Without another payoff, he disappeared. Tom and I cared enough to console each other when we ended our relationship.

  But sometimes this kind of honesty is not possible. In an abusive relationship, the wisest action is to write the person a letter that you will *not* send, expressing your feelings without putting yourself at risk.

- *Perform your own ritual of completion.* Find a ritual that works for you. Recently, my friend Ben's mother died after living with him for years and requiring constant care. Cleaning out her room became his ritual of completion. He spent time by himself going through her closet and dresser, giving away her clothing to friends and charitable organizations. He sorted through her papers, finding old cards and photographs that brought back happy memories. Sifting through years of feelings, he decided what to keep and what to discard. Then he gave away her old bedroom set, painted the room, and bought a desk, bookshelves, and sofa bed, setting up a new study and guest room. When he was finished, Ben took a trip back to his old neighborhood in New York, walking around and reviewing his memories. All of this was his way of saying good-bye, a ritual of respect and release.

Sometimes when we perform honorable closure we feel a heavy weight being lifted from our shoulders. At other times, there's a bittersweet sense of an ending. But it's important to be aware of life's changes, to honor these times of transition. Essential to weaving the pattern of our lives, closure helps us bind off one experience in order to move on to another. It remains in the few rites of passage that endure in our culture: ceremonies for graduations, weddings, funerals, and christenings. With honorable closure, mindful individuals honor the conclusions and commencements in their lives. Aware of their timing, they create their own patterns of meaning with power and grace.

## Pointers for Greater Power and Peace

*Here are some ways to create better timing in your life.*

■ *Practice better time-management habits.*

- Don't stretch yourself too thin, filling your time with too many commitments.
- Don't take on too many things to prove you're strong.
- Remember to delegate whenever you can.
- Learn to prioritize and pace yourself.
- Don't subordinate yourself to a job or relationship.
- Don't cut your margins too thin.
- Use *ma-ai* to see things in perspective.

■ *Practice* **musubi** *to avoid procrastination.*

- Use momentum. Get started and keep moving.
- Don't worry. Do something, even if it's only making a list.
- Break a difficult task into smaller sections and attack one at a time.
- Develop your own system to handle routine work.
- Use different speeds for different projects and know when to shift.

■ *Remember to practice honorable closure when a cycle is ending.*

- Know when and how to let go with honesty and respect for yourself and the other person(s).
- Practice a ritual of formal release.

# The Lesson of Courage

Go within,

Focus your senses,

Face the challenge.

Balance sunlight and shadow.

Blend with the path.

This is the way of Tao.

*TAO, 56* [1]

腹

The courage of Tao is not so much external as internal, not so much the courage to climb Mount Everest as the courage to live your own life. Each of us knows how it feels when we have the courage to follow our hearts, to live our convictions. We've all felt the sense of personal power that comes from simultaneously reaching out to new experience and reaching in to a deeper sense of ourselves, a spirit of adventure that dates back to when we were young girls.[2]

I remember afternoons exploring the hills around Hamilton Air Force Base in northern California when I was nine years old. With my blond pigtails flying, my pocketknife and rabbit's foot hanging from my belt, and a few Tootsie Rolls in my pocket, I'd go off with my friends Joan and Shorty and Shorty's dog, Poochie, who he swore was half coyote. We'd wander up and down, exploring creeks and caves, climbing to the hilltops, looking down at the valley below. Collecting feathers and rocks and looking for arrowheads, we'd tell stories, pretending we were Indian braves.

Climbing trees was my own private adventure. Sometimes I'd sit for hours in the redwood tree beside my house, sheltered by the dense green branches, embraced by the fragrance of pine. Higher and higher I'd go, up one branch and around the next until I reached my favorite perch. Then I'd look down at the red tile roof of our two-story house, down at my parents' window far below, and up, like a bird, at the bright blue sky overhead.

I'd see Shorty's house next door, a mirror image of ours. The sounds of his mother in the kitchen would be followed by the aroma of her spaghetti sauce wafting up through the treetops on the afternoon breeze. There were times of silence with only the sounds of birds singing in the boughs overhead and the soft wind whispering through the trees. Long afternoons blended into evenings when the parting sun painted the sky and a lone bugle played taps, as life on the military base marked the end of another day.

I used to love climbing trees, looking down from their amazing heights. As a nine-year-old girl, so much of my life had to do with looking up: at parents, teachers, authority figures, rules and regulations. Here at least, I could rise by my own efforts, one with the mighty redwood tree. At other bases my friends and I built tree forts, sat high in the branches like sailors on the masts of gallant square-riggers, looking for pirates in our imagination. But I don't remember anyone else sharing that redwood tree. It was associated in my mind with my first feelings of competence, climbing under my own power. I recall my delight at being so far above the house with all its chores. For a little girl growing up on Air Force bases, always packing up and following my father to new assignments, climbing a tree was something I could do on my own, a quiet affirmation of courage that put me that much closer to the sky.

## WHAT ARE WE AFRAID OF NOW?

THE YEARS go by, clouding the brave spirits of our childhood with layers of fears and inhibitions. We become anxious, hesitant, reluctant to live our own adventures, to become most fully ourselves.

What are we afraid of? Psychologists say many women hold themselves back, unwilling to say or do as they wish because they fear rejection and abandonment. Reaching out to discover more about ourselves and our world, once so natural in childhood, now seems dangerous, a threat to our security. We come up against a barrier of fear, not fear of failure but fear of developing our own competence, which may alienate those we love.[3]

This barrier inhibits our personal growth, shifting our attention as we approach adolescence from success in academic and athletic pursuits to a craving for acceptance and an obsession with our appearance. Eclipsing our earlier sense of personal power, our social conditioning gradually convinces us to be less than what we are. We get debilitating messages, not only from the fashion industry but from well-meaning adults who subtly reinforce us for "safe" limits of self-expression. In the sixth grade, my friend Barbara wanted to be a mathematician and I wanted to be an astrophysicist. She got a Ph.D. in history and I got one in English because our teachers told us girls don't do things like math and science. We hope her daughter, Katie, now eleven, will be able to stay on course and follow her dreams.

The threshold of adulthood too often narrows the lives of young girls within prescribed "feminine" limits. We fear extending our power and stop reaching out for new possibilities because of what others may think.

Too many of us become *rubricized*, reduced to a function, identified not in terms of who we are but what we do. Psychologist Jean Baker Miller says, "Our culture tends to 'objectify' people, that is, to treat most people as if they were things; it treats women almost totally in this way."[4]

We learn to anticipate the wishes of others, to react instead of to act. Following a carefully conditioned choreography in our relationships, we learn to dance backward, taking our steps in reaction to those of our partners, who invariably take the lead. And we do this reactive dance not only with the men in our lives but with our parents, children, friends, and coworkers. Responding, not initiating, we live much of our lives in anticipation of others' wishes.

We do this because we want to earn their love. And some of us really go to extremes. When Jane started dating Jeff, she did everything she could to win his affection. She bought him new shirts, ties, and an expensive wallet, called him nearly every day, left notes and homemade cookies on his doorstep. She dropped by unannounced or parked outside his house waiting for him to come home so she could surprise him with a home-cooked meal. In the beginning, Jeff was flattered by all the attention, but then he began to feel smothered. Every time he turned around there was a card, a gift, a note from Jane. It was too much. Despite—or rather because of—all her efforts, he told her he didn't want to see her again.

Psychologists point out that no matter how hard we try, we cannot win love by making ourselves indispensable because people do *not* love out of obligation. This principle applies not only to women like Jane, but also to self-sacrificing wives and mothers. According to Jean Baker Miller, people "may become dependent on [our] services, but that is different from real interest and love. In fact, if men and children become too dependent, they can come to feel trapped by their dependency, and come to hate the person who is taking care of them so well."[5] Ironically, then, we are most loved when we are most fully ourselves and able to accept a corresponding wholeness in others. In other words, we can have real relationships only by being real people, not by being repressed and rubricized.

Holding ourselves back, living in anticipation of others' needs is both unproductive and unhealthy. Abraham Maslow once said, "If you deliberately set out to be less than you are capable of, you'll be unhappy for the rest of your life."[6] The *Tao Te Ching* tells us:

*Wise women who follow the Tao*
*Do not worry about others' business*
*Or judge themselves by others' standards.*
*Living simply,*
*They honor their own patterns.*
TAO, 65

# *B*UILDING YOUR COURAGE

IT DOES not take a major life change to reclaim the sense of power and adventure you felt as a young girl. You can begin right where you are, building your courage the same way you can build your stamina—with the right kind of exercise.

Human beings *need* challenge. We also need security. And each of us requires a different balance of the two. Too much change and uncertainty can overwhelm us. Too much monotony and we become bored and restless. Challenge and security, power and peace, are essential to life. The lessons of centering and simplicity from earlier chapters will increase your peace of mind. In this chapter you will learn to use your challenges as exercises to develop your courage.

Courage for women today means many things. It is an attitude, a state of mind. It means being able:

- to be yourself, without imitation or apology.
- to take the first step in a new direction.
- to tell the truth.
- to love unconditionally.
- to speak up in your own authentic voice.
- to dare to disagree.
- to deal with conflict honestly.
- to face your fears and learn from them.
- to move through life with vitality and confidence.

We can build our courage by developing our competence. Studies of U.S. astronauts have shown that their competence—their coordination, intelligence, and expertise as pilots—increases their courage when they face the unknown. Instead of fear, many astronauts experience a sense of power and exhilaration when preparing for flights into outer space. They feel they can handle any challenge because they've developed a personal pattern of success.[7]

Developing a sense of mastery in one field can lead you to greater success in other areas. This is because, like the astronauts, you learn to believe in yourself, developing the skill of working through challenges, one vital step at a time. An important step in this process is facing your fears.

### WHAT WE LEARN BY FACING OUR FEARS

Social psychologists treat abnormal fears, or phobias (fear of open spaces, fear of dogs, fear of flying), with a process of *desensitization*, gradual exposure to more and more of the fearful stimulus.[8] Becoming more familiar with the perceived threat and realizing they can handle it helps people gain confidence and overcome their fears.

Facing your fears and learning from them will help you develop greater courage as well. Fear is your body's natural warning system, telling you to pay attention—you may be in danger. "What's the real risk here?" and "What am I really afraid of?" are important questions to ask. Many people experience fear whenever they face new challenges.

### HOW DO YOU DEFINE THE STRESS RESPONSE?

Anxiety in any new situation is normal. But psychologist Tracey Kahan says that most men in our society are raised to push through their comfort zones while most women draw back as soon as they feel uncomfortable. How you define this discomfort determines how you respond to it.[9] In an unfamiliar situation, most people experience the stress response: accelerated heartbeat, release of adrenaline throughout the body, tense muscles, and other physiological reactions associated with fight or flight.

When you're in a challenging situation—speaking in public, going on a job interview, facing the unknown—and you feel that familiar adrenaline rush, what do you call it?

- fear
- anxiety
- the jitters
- stage fright
- nervousness
- excitement
- energy

What you're feeling is heightened awareness, a surge of energy. What's the difference between fear and excitement? Perhaps it's just your point of view.

## *M*OVING BEYOND FEAR

STUDIES HAVE shown that young girls who participate in sports are less fearful than girls who don't. There's something empowering about using our bodies actively, testing our limits, falling down and getting up again. Realizing that we can work through injuries and failures, make fools of ourselves and survive, builds our confidence and personal power.

Before getting her Ph.D. in psychology, Tracey Kahan was a ski instructor in Taos, New Mexico. She often taught the beginners' classes, which were mostly women. Outfitted in colorful ski clothes, with rented skis, boots, and poles, some women were still not fully present.

"Why are you taking this class?" Tracey would ask, and learned that many were there with their husbands or boyfriends who really loved to ski. The women were taking skiing lessons because they thought they *should*. Women do lots of things to please others. But skiing requires intense commitment and should never be done half-heartedly.

"Skiing is a very physically risky activity. If you are not here for yourself, don't do it," she told them. And some women would take off their skis and go into town to shop or visit art galleries. For those who remained, skiing was an empowering personal exercise, a way to face their fears, learning the difference between social anxiety and physical danger.

When you recognize the kind of fear you're dealing with, you can respond to it more effectively. With *social anxiety*, the "danger" is only looking foolish to others. Yet such anxiety keeps many people from learning new skills because they're afraid of making mistakes in public. This is especially true for women, Tracey says, since "we're used to defining ourselves as others see us." Whenever we do anything new, we come up against an emotional checkpoint—fear of failure and social embarrassment—which must be overcome before moving on to greater accomplishment. We *must* be willing to make mistakes, to get back up and try again.

Learning from our fears means becoming more aware of our bodies, modifying our responses to deal successfully with the challenges we face. We naturally tense up in response to stress, but this tension often gets in our way. Since tense muscles make people more susceptible to injury, Tracey taught her students to relax, let go, and laugh when they fell down in the snow. Before I give public lectures, I take a deep breath and gradually release it, focusing my energy on the task at hand.

Tracey says that the greatest challenge for most women is "figuring out where they are in their bodies." When we lack a sense of physical competence, we are naturally more fearful and reactive. One step at a time, she would teach her students to know their bodies, their abilities, to move around in their skis, to do a snowplow stop and turn, to take longer and longer runs. "To know your body is to know yourself," she says.

## ℱACING NEW CHALLENGES

OUR BODIES and our emotions are intimately connected. Working with our body's wisdom helps us understand ourselves at a deeper level, learning from our fears, not only on the ski slopes but in the daily challenges of our lives. With awareness comes power. By becoming more aware of your own responses and using the strategies that follow, you can transform any challenge into an opportunity for greater insight and empowerment.

- *Recognize the adrenaline response and use it to advantage.* Remember, fear is just a rush of energy that can help focus your attention. Ask, "What's the real risk here?" Is it a social anxiety or a physical threat? Then choose the best response.
- *Don't freeze up. Stay focused.* Fear can paralyze or mobilize you. Since you cannot be tense and relaxed at the same time, do a relaxation technique: Take a deep breath and let it out with a "whoosh." Use positive imaging or an affirmation. Tell yourself, "I *can* handle this."
- *Get clear on what you want to do.* Before attempting a new run, Tracey sizes up the situation, asking, "Where do I want to go?" Before taking action, get a clear idea of your goal.
- *Evaluate the conditions.* Ski runs can vary from day to day—

it could have snowed last night or the trails might be icy. Melting snow may have exposed hazardous rocks or tree branches. On the ski slope or in life, knowing what you have to face can help you take the right action. What are the conditions like for you?

- *Don't concentrate on what you want to avoid.* People often get fixated on hazards. Tracey knows from skiing that if she concentrates on the sharp rocks jutting out at the end of a trail, she'll run right into them. She acknowledges the danger, then plots her course beyond it, looking where she wants to go. Don't fixate on obstacles and visualize failure. Take hazards into account, but keep your eyes on your goal.

- *After considering the conditions, ask yourself if you're ready to take this risk.* This means knowing yourself, your capabilities and your current condition. How are you feeling? Are you focused and confident? Tired? Are you up to this challenge? If so, continue. If you're not ready, then get out.

- *Choose a course of action and follow through.* If you've said yes to the challenge, then follow through to the best of your ability. If you've said no, find a way to withdraw. Either way, commit to your choice of action, remaining centered so you can make adjustments if new conditions arise.

- *When you've completed the action, congratulate yourself and review the results.* You did it! Now, what did you learn about the situation? About yourself? How can you use this insight next time?

You can get back in touch with the adventurous self of your girlhood and build your personal power by exercising your courage. Whether it's developing a new skill or improving your athletic ability, you'll find yourself learning from your successes and failures and living with greater vitality.

# ✳ECOMING YOUR OWN HERO

THROUGHOUT HISTORY, legend, and literature, most of our heroes have been men. Dictionaries and reference books routinely define a hero as "a man who" overcomes obstacles, performs extraordinary acts of courage, or is the main character in a novel or drama.[10] It's time we realized that women can be heroes. When we reach out to embrace the power of our potential and become more authentically ourselves, we become the heroes of our own lives.

Each of us has her own ideals of courageous womanhood. I think of Eleanor Roosevelt, Golda Meir, Amelia Earhart, Margaret Sanger, Sacajawea, Sojourner Truth, Louisa May Alcott, Marie Curie, Georgia O'Keeffe, Margaret Mead, and Barbara Jordan. Women in sport, like world champion runner Florence Griffith Joyner, jockey Robyn Smith, and ultra marathon runner Ann Trason, give us new models of power and endurance. Who are some women you admire?

## ROLE MODELS IN LIFE WRITING

The lives of heroic women cast long shadows, showing what you, too, may accomplish. This week, go to a bookstore or library and get a biography of a woman you admire. If you don't have someone in mind, ask your local librarian or browse in the biography or women's studies section. Read some of the new memoirs about early American women or learn about a woman from your own cultural background. Find out how she overcame life's challenges, developed her character, created a new image of what women can be.

The life of a woman of courage can take many forms. There is the courage of an astronaut or the courage of a woman on the frontier, building her life's dream in a new

land. There's the quiet courage of a woman of integrity and the moral courage of one who dares to live for truth.

One model of courage for our time is Aung San Suu Kyi, the leader of the democracy movement in Burma. Affirming her own personal power in the face of oppression, this woman has confronted angry crowds, lived under house arrest, faced government soldiers armed with guns and bayonets. With quiet dignity she has walked through barricades and spoken eloquently, upholding a vision of freedom for her people. One of her speeches contains these lines about facing fear:

"You should not let your fears prevent you from doing what you know is right. Not that you shouldn't be afraid. Fear is normal. But to be inhibited from doing what you know is right, that is what is dangerous. You should be able to lead your life in the right way—despite your fears."[11]

In 1991, Aung San Suu Kyi was awarded the Nobel Prize for Peace. She remains a heroic example to all women, affirming that we can face our fears with courage and transform the challenges of our lives with our own creative power.

■ *Choose your own practice of courage.*

- Is there a skill you'd like to develop or a weakness you'd like to overcome?
- Make yourself a plan. Sign up for a class, join a support group, get some information at your local library.
- When you begin to face this new challenge, recognize the adrenaline response and develop a strategy for dealing with it. Take a deep breath. Say an affirmation to yourself.
- Get clear on what you want to do. Stay focused on your goal. Visualize yourself already achieving it.
- Evaluate the conditions. What do you need to do now?
- Don't concentrate on what you want to avoid or picture yourself failing. Worry can actually work *against* you as a self-fulfilling prophecy.
- See yourself succeeding. Keep your visualizations *positive*. Then ask yourself what you need to get there.
- Ask yourself if you are ready to take action. If so, *do* it, to the best of your ability—and enjoy the process.

■ *Study the life of a woman you admire.*

Go to the library or bookstore and get her biography. Ask yourself these questions and write down the answers:

- What do I admire most about her?
- What qualities do I find most heroic?

- How did she express these qualities?
- What is *one* quality of hers I'd like to develop more of myself?
- How can I do this?

Your answers can help you design a new practice of courage for yourself. Following the steps in the previous exercise, make yourself a plan to increase your personal power by developing more of the quality you admire.

# *The Lesson of Strength*

Combine the assertive strength of

*yang*

With the heart of compassionate

*yin*.

In this valley of possibilities,

Live your life like a river,

Strong and true,

Renewing your spirit

With the power of nature,

The wisdom of Tao.

*TAO, 28*

*W*hat does it mean to be a strong woman? One evening last November, I drove to my aikido dojo to meet someone who would know. Sue Ann McKean, a fourth-degree black belt and former world-class bodybuilder, would be a guest instructor that night. What would she be like, I wondered—muscular, imposing, supremely confident? I was curious and intimidated.

When I entered the dojo, the class had already begun. Clad in her white *gi* and black *hakama,* with her sandy hair pulled back in a long braid, Sue Ann was demonstrating a technique. Pausing in the doorway, I watched in amazement. This woman moved with consummate grace. Combining the focused power of *yang* with the flexibility of *yin,* her movements flowed like water, transcending my expectations. She embodied a new definition of strength that blended both extremes.

After class, I wanted to know more. How had she learned this? Impressed by her openness and ready smile, I walked over to join Sue Ann for tea and conversation beside the mat.

"My father was a Marine," she told me. She'd grown up on military bases where men were the warriors, women and children "dependents." It didn't take Sue Ann long to realize she was "really low in the pecking order, being a girl."

To overcome her sense of powerlessness, as a teenager she began studying karate. "It felt good to get out my frustrations, to feel my muscles and do something with my tension," she said. But as a girl in a class full of GIs, Sue Ann was "really getting banged up a lot." Karate could be empowering but the force and competition were alienating her from herself, so she tried t'ai chi but found it too slow. Then she found aikido and saw "all these opposites coming together: sensitivity and power, grace and strength, a kind of compassionate power."

Sue Ann earned an aikido black belt, but found herself living a contradiction. Aikido philosophy is all about finding your own center, but she was still deferring to her teacher, "making the center outside myself." If he said something different from what she felt, she denied her own feelings, concluding that he was right, she was wrong. "That kind of thinking," she said, "is giving your power away."

Now when Sue Ann teaches aikido, she works to prevent this loss of power for her students. When she demonstrates techniques, she tells students to make them their own, listen to their bodies, trust themselves, and follow their own inner teacher. "How do we awaken the teacher in the students?" is a question she asks herself often.

Sue Ann's story about giving power away shows how we become like submissive children when we defer to others. How often we make others our judges. Yet, ultimately, who can decide for us what is right and wrong? A wise woman respects others but always follows her own heart.

After a few years in aikido, Sue Ann began lifting weights, which led her into professional bodybuilding. "I learned what true strength is and it's *not* what you think it is," she said with a smile.

"The healthy way," she explained, is to lift weights "for process, to be present, to be more connected." But after a while, she got "caught up in the appearance, the competition. My body became this object that had to be sculpted, perfected, oiled and tanned and fed and supplemented and trained and put to bed in this rigid way. So I *looked* extremely strong—that's the irony of it. I looked very strong and *felt* extremely weak, very vulnerable. My body fat was down to five percent. I was starving all the time."

The bodybuilding competitions made Sue Ann realize how she'd been setting herself up for judgment all her life. "Imagine you're an artist and your materials are your flesh and blood and bones and then you've got to display the art to five thousand people," she said. "And the judges would be going down the line, looking us over. There's no soul, no being, no spirit there—just these hunks of flesh, checking out the biceps. I was so dissociated. I felt like a slave being auctioned off."

Bodybuilding, she realized, "isn't about strength. It's about image and presentation. I came out in front of all these people in my *bathing suit,* in this little teeny posing suit, saying to them, 'Do you love me? Do you like me?' " She shook her head at how this mirrored the drama she'd been playing all her life.

Finally, Sue Ann found the strength she'd been looking for. Strength for her means being vulnerable and being okay with her own vulnerability, a deep lesson in self-acceptance no one could give her but herself.

"I spent a lot of my life trying to be a *something,*" she said. "Being a world-class bodybuilder. Being a strong martial artist." But whenever she gets "into controlling too much, making things matter too much, pushing my weight around," she gets injured. Sue Ann sees this as a wake-up call, reminding her to stop focusing so much on externals and honor her own process.

We don't have to become martial artists or world-class bodybuilders to learn this lesson. The mistake too many of us make, whether it's in our training, our appearance, our careers, or our relationships, is trying to get strength externally.

Sue Ann used to think that if she pumped iron, she was going to be strong. "And I pumped iron. Boy, did I pump iron! I had huge muscles but I did not *feel* strong. Seeking something extrinsically—if we seek it for the image, for the prestige, it's not real strength. It's not real power. It's just show."

Real strength is self-acceptance. It's letting go, becoming one with the process, whatever we're doing, for what it can teach us about ourselves, for the joy of doing it, for the power of the present moment.

Sue Ann McKean is still exploring her own definition of strength. An important part of her journey is bodywork. To balance her many *yang* activities—teaching aikido, lifting weights—she practices therapeutic massage, using her strength to nurture others with the power of touch. It's her way of expressing the *yin* energy too often discounted by our culture, which defines power as force, competition, and domination.

"In order to survive," she says, many women "take on the male, macho model of power." Sue Ann finds this "a kind of betrayal, costing so much to the essence of me." So she seeks to discover her "feminine strength, the power of being receptive and open and empty. But," she asked, shrugging her shoulders, "what in our culture supports *that*?"

In developing our strength as women we are in uncharted territory. Our culture offers us few role models. "What's feminine power?" asked Sue Ann wistfully. "After thousands of years of suppressing feminine energy, nobody knows what that is." It's a mystery for each woman to solve for herself.[1]

Feminine power is a mystery for our society as well, one we must solve for the health and wholeness of humanity. For far too long, we have upheld the aggressive, masculine extreme as our model of power and achievement. According to psychiatrist Jean Baker Miller, "We have reached the end of the road that is built on the set of traits held out for male identity—advance at any cost, pay any price, drive out all competitors, and kill them if necessary."[2]

Cultural crises and personal quests converge in a solution as old as the *Tao*, as new as today. Each of us has the strength of *yin* and the strength of *yang*, the traditional "feminine" strength of nurturing and compassion as well as the more assertive strength of *yang*, the ability to go after what we want. No longer are women expected to be merely "chaste, silent, and obedient," like the ideal woman of the English Renaissance.[3] No longer must either man or woman be limited to half the strength in our human repertoire. Each of us can claim for herself the strength to be whole, to develop her personal power to the best of her ability.

## ℰLAIMING OUR POWER

CLAIMING OUR personal power begins with redefining it. Too often, people associate power with something outside themselves. This is "positional power," rooted in externals: rank, job, financial status, the trappings of authority. Many of us feel weak and intimidated around people with more positional power. But we no longer live in a world with divine-right monarchy, when aristocrats were considered somehow closer to God. Positional power is limited and temporary. It is the series of uniforms people wear, beneath which we are all human beings. When people lose their jobs or retire, they also lose their positional power.

The other kind of power, the kind that lasts, is personal power. This is the power that makes you who you are: your energy, your values, your integrity and spiritual strength. Throughout history, people have exercised moral leadership with the force of personal power, people such as Mohandas Gandhi, Albert Schweitzer, Eleanor Roosevelt, Helen Caldicott, Mother Teresa. Who they were transcended rank or title, giving meaning to their lives and inspiring those around them.

Following the Tao of womanhood, we can build our personal power by becoming more aware of what we value. As we clarify our vision, our choices become spiritual exercises.

Becoming more mindful, we learn to avoid detours, attitudes and actions that drain the power from our lives. One detour is holding ourselves back because we don't want to be "selfish." This traps us in a reductive false dilemma in which we feel that exercising our power means depriving someone else—either/or, all or nothing, us or them, you or me. But life is very rarely that simple. Choosing *for* yourself need not mean choosing *against* someone else. It may open up new possibilities for everyone.

Lyn and Rick are two people who've created a new life for themselves, drawing upon the strengths of *both* of them. Rick is a writer and former college professor who left his academic job to found his own magazine. Lyn is a resourceful woman and an expert skier. A few years ago, they lived in North Carolina, where Rick edited his magazine. Now they spend winters in Colorado and the rest of the year in North Carolina. During the winter, Lyn spends her days on the ski patrol while Rick writes. He's now finishing his second novel. In the spring, they return to North Carolina, where Rick manages a land trust devoted to protecting the environment while Lyn works as a carpenter. She has written a book on home repair for women, which was published last year. Either/or has nothing to do with Lyn and Rick's life, which is a beautiful synthesis of *both* their strengths.[4]

Another detour to avoid is learned submissive behavior. Too many women are conditioned as girls to be submissive and dependent. They play up to people in power with an attitude of helplessness designed to please adults, especially men.[5] We've all known women who trade on being helpless. One woman I knew was convinced she couldn't change a lightbulb and had to call her father over whenever one burned out. Another had to call her boyfriend to hang the pictures in her new apartment because she didn't know how to use a hammer. Then there are women like Lyn, who create lives of power and fulfillment, transcending old stereotypes with dynamic new definitions of what women can be.

## THE POWER OF *YANG:* EXTENDING *KI*

YOU CAN develop greater personal power by becoming more aware of your *ki.* Martial artists can overcome opponents three times their size, break bricks with their bare hands, and throw another person across the room—all with the power of *ki. Ki* in Japanese (*ch'i* in Chinese) is your vital energy, your life force. When you are optimistic, you naturally extend *ki,* your immune system works more effectively, and you move with power and grace. We've all felt that vitality when we were filled with positive *ki.*

When your *ki* is low, you lack judgment and confidence, are reactive and vulnerable to manipulation. You lower your *ki* with self-defeating habits like:

- doubting yourself
- "needing" someone's approval
- thinking negatively about yourself or others
- subordinating yourself to someone you love or admire
- subordinating yourself to your work
- holding yourself back, afraid of not being "ladylike"
- making self-deprecating remarks
- denying yourself adequate rest and recreation

How do you feel when you're caught in one of these self-defeating patterns? Chances are you're tired and run down because you've exhausted your *ki.*

Like the electrical energy in a battery, your *ki* can be depleted or recharged. Sleep deprivation, one of the hazards of our busy lives, drains our *ki,* compromises our immune system, and makes us anxious and reactive. If you've been feeling worried and anxious, you can begin recharging your energy and improving your attitude by simply giving yourself a good night's sleep.

You can also strengthen your *ki* with a more positive attitude. Negative thinking undermines us in ways too numerous to mention. Think weakness and you become weak. Think strength, increase your *ki,* and you'll become more successful at everything you do.

You can strengthen your *ki* by extending it—by reaching out with deliberate intention. News reports are filled with stories of women who demonstrated remarkable strength in a crisis, carrying a loved one to safety or lifting a heavy automobile to save an injured child, because their intention was so focused. This same one-pointed intention gives martial artists the strength to break bricks or throw heavy opponents.

Intention can keep us going until we reach our goals. How often do students and teachers get sick at the end of a term when the last exam is over? Or how many busy women collapse during the holidays after the last gift is wrapped? Their intention has been carrying them. Once they reach their goal, they stop extending their *ki* and collapse. A better way would be to recharge your *ki* regularly when you're entering a stressful period, then nurture yourself afterward, taking time to relax and remembering to get a good night's sleep.

Here are some ways to recharge your *ki* on a regular basis:

- by eating a balanced diet with lots of fresh fruits and vegetables
- by exercising, which improves your circulation and oxygenates your blood, cleaning out your system from within
- by play, which relaxes you and improves your circulation
- by singing, letting your voice extend outward in joy
- by going to places with good associations—your favorite art gallery, park, or cathedral. My aikido dojo is such a place. When I'm there, I'm always glad to be alive.
- by smiling. Psychologists have found that the simple act of smiling sends a message to your brain to become more positive and energized.[6]
- by *misogi* breathing, which cleanses the system

## *M*ISOGI BREATHING

*MISOGI*, AS we learned in Chapter 4, is ritualistic cleansing or purification. To renew their *ki*, martial artists often conclude their training with *misogi* breathing.

To perform your own *misogi* breathing, sit on the floor cross-legged or sit in a straight-backed chair with your hands on your thighs, palms down.

Relax your body and feel your weight solidly on the surface beneath you.

Close your eyes and slowly breathe out through your mouth, making silently the sound "ha."

Now slowly breathe in through your nose while focusing on the *hara* or point of power, right beneath your navel. As you breathe in, think silently to yourself, "Power."

Feel the power of *ki* fill your body.

Repeat the slow out breath and the in breath two more times.

Finish with a long, final out breath.

Open your eyes.

Often, after an aikido class, we do *misogi* breathing for ten or fifteen minutes. Zen Buddhists sit and meditate on their breathing for hours. You can do *misogi* breathing—with your eyes open—during your lunch hour, waiting for an appointment, even while stuck in traffic. Find time to recharge your *ki* each day. Go outside during lunch and practice *ki* breathing while watching the world go by. You can renew your power this way whenever you give yourself the chance. It's as close as your next breath.

## THE POWER OF *YIN*: YOUR INNER STRENGTH AND WISDOM

OUR ACTIVE, competitive culture rewards the strength of *yang* much more than the strength of *yin*. Yet Eastern wisdom has long acknowledged the power of water, which is gentle and nurturing, but can cut through solid rock.

## THE STRENGTH OF HUMILITY

THE *TAO* tells us, "Those who know they do not know become wise" (*Tao*, 71).[7] The *yin* strength of recognizing what we do not know opens us up to new insight. Pretense only weakens us.

After working in sales, Sarah was excited about her job interview at a science research lab. Here was a chance for a stable job on the beautiful University of Wisconsin campus. She loved the atmosphere, the hours, the people she met. There was only one problem: the job description said "word processing," and Sarah had never used a computer. Still, she figured, she could learn. When Dr. Steinmann, the department head, asked her about computer skills, she said, "Sure, I can do it," which seemed to satisfy him. She got the job and moved into her new office on Monday morning, meeting all the researchers, who seemed like a congenial group. Dr. Steinmann even told her to call him "Marty."

But there, on the desk, sat the computer. Wondering what to do, she sat in her office as the researchers came in with memos, reports, and grant proposals. She turned on the computer but couldn't figure out how to open a file or even get into the word processing program. Each day she sat in her office and the stack of papers on her desk grew higher. Marty came in asking about his report and other researchers dropped by to pick up their memos and proposals. "I'm just finishing it up. I'll have it to you right away," Sarah said to them, becoming more and more frantic. The next week the pile of paperwork grew. Still no results. Soon it was clear to everyone that she couldn't do the work and she received her termination notice.

Had she had the strength of humility, Sarah could have taken a word-processing course to prepare for the kind of job she wanted.

Being honest about what we do *not* know can empower us to seek the truth. In 1969, a young woman's curiosity led her to spend long days in the basement of the Berkeley agricultural library, reading whatever she could find on U.S. farming, plant proteins, human nutrition, and world hunger. She was not an expert, not even a scientist, but there was a lot she wanted to learn. That young woman was Frances Moore Lappé and the result of her research was *Diet for a Small Planet*,[8] a breakthrough study that proposed an innovative solution to world hunger—increasing available food by decreasing our dependence upon meat, combining plant proteins, and eating lower on the food chain. Her approach revealed a solution the experts had failed to see and demonstrated what one person who does not know can do when she has the courage to follow her own questions.

## THE STRENGTH OF PERSEVERANCE

ANOTHER IMPORTANT *yin* strength is perseverance. The way you handle resistance can make a major difference in your life. Many people give up when faced with a difficult task. Others try to push through impatiently with the strength of *yang*.

Many students today are sophisticated when it comes to computers and mass media but lack the strength of perseverance. When they can't understand a difficult assignment, they give up and stop reading. Or they skip the difficult passages and rush to the end of the chapter. Neither way leads to understanding.

But there is another way, the way of perseverance. With enough time and concentrated effort, a mountain stream can cut through solid rock. With enough time and perseverance, you can overcome resistance if you remember to:

- Slow down.
- Not get overwhelmed and frantic.
- Continue to move ahead, slowly and steadily.
- Watch for openings and breakthroughs.

These principles work well, whether you're studying a difficult subject, learning a new skill, or dealing with difficult people.

If you don't understand something you're reading, slow

down. Reread the passage. Focus on the details and important concepts. Look up words you don't understand. Ask questions. Make sure you comprehend the first section before moving on to section two. Keep moving forward, one step at a time, until you break through resistance to greater understanding.

When we're learning a new skill, there's usually an initial burst of enthusiasm and sense of progress. Then at some point we all hit a plateau. Two teenage girls in my aikido class just hit their first plateau. When they started training, they learned quickly. But one night after class, they were both complaining in the dressing room.

As she put away her *gi,* Janeen looked down at the floor and said, "I don't feel like I'm getting anywhere at all. I feel like giving up."

"That's how I feel," said Michelle. "When I first came, I felt I was learning something, but now I don't feel like I'm doing any good at all."

But they were. They no longer looked like beginners. With their ponytails flying, they were taking falls and rolling with precision and balance. Their techniques were getting smoother and stronger. But they couldn't see it.

Aikido instructor and psychologist George Leonard says that all athletes learn in a stair-step pattern, with a leap of progress followed by a flat period in which they feel they aren't learning anything at all, and then, finally, another breakthrough and leap ahead. The path of mastery, as he calls it, is sustained only by those who can persevere through the plateaus, learning to love the process itself without being driven by results.[9]

When you're learning a new skill and hit a plateau, don't let impatience overwhelm you. Slow down. Focus on the process. Pay attention to the individual steps and stop judging yourself so much. Watch. Listen. Get your ego out of the way. When you're ready for a breakthrough, it will come. As Shakespeare said in *Hamlet*, "the readiness is all." Sometimes, all we can do—when we don't know what else to do—is to be mindful of the process and persevere.

## THE STRENGTH OF COMPASSION

ANOTHER IMPORTANT *yin* strength is compassion, the power that comes from being open and receptive. We exercise compassion by slowing down to listen to others, giving them our attention while opening ourselves up to the power of insight. Practicing this skill requires us to be mindful. If we're open and receptive at the wrong time with the wrong person, we can get hurt. But extending the strength of compassion connects us to a powerful source of wisdom.

Compassion can cut through resistance, bringing greater understanding and revealing new solutions. Jane Curry is a political science professor specializing in the politics of Eastern Europe. She also practices the politics of compassion. For over twenty years she has done research in Poland. With her ability to listen and speak from the heart, she has won the respect of government officials on all sides, producing not only a series of impressive books but an extended family of enduring relationships. At her university she also combines the personal with the political, practicing compassion with students, who often come to her for advice. When she learned one student was homeless and living in his car, she went to the college president, who got him a special scholarship. Extending her compassion into the community, she serves on the board of the local homeless shelter. In her lively household, friends, colleagues, students, and an occasional visitor from Poland often join Jane and her three children around the dinner table to share their stories.[10] Her life reminds me of a favorite quote from the *Tao Te Ching:*

> *Nothing in the world*
> *Is more gentle than water*
> *Yet nothing is stronger.*
> *Water nurtures life*
> *Yet cuts through solid rock.*
> *Overcome obstacles*
> *With the strength of gentleness.*
> TAO, 78

## THE STRENGTH OF INTUITION

THE FINAL *yin* strength is intuition, the quiet wisdom that comes from deep within us. It is a connection between actions and individuals that transcends what our rational minds can know, providing a flash of insight, an unexpected solution, a living link with family and loved ones. How often have you successfully followed a "hunch," or felt you should call someone and found the person really needed to talk to you?

There are many explanations for what has been called "women's intuition." Some say it is our brain chemistry, our responsibility for nurturing others, or our exclusion from the male power structure. Some people offer metaphysical explanations while others say intuition comes from the brain's ability to think in probabilities, arranging past experience into predictable patterns. Whatever the cause, intuition can be a tremendous source of strength. As a supplement to conscious thought, it provides us with valuable insights and unforeseen possibilities.

The summer I was nineteen, I worked at a temporary agency before returning to college. While driving through downtown Riverside one afternoon in August, I passed the *Press-Enterprise* newspaper office. On sudden impulse, I turned my red Volkswagen into the parking lot and walked inside.

"Hello," I said to the woman at the front desk. "My name is Diane Dreher and I'm studying to be a writer. I'd like to apply for a job." She ushered me back to the personnel office, where I filled out an application. Then I was taken up to the newsroom to meet my new boss.

By amazing coincidence, the *Press-Enterprise*'s college intern had given her notice that morning and I had walked into her job. The next week I reported for work. The job was perfect for me. Just a short drive from the university, the newsroom was a fascinating place, open day and night so I could work around my class schedule. I supported myself during college and gained valuable experience. Another student who worked there became a lifelong friend.

What made me go into the newspaper office that day? Nothing my conscious mind knew about. I wasn't thinking of applying for jobs, and even if I had been, the newspaper hadn't advertised the position yet. It had to be intuition, divine guidance, or synchronicity that connected me with this job.

### DEVELOPING YOUR INTUITION

You can use your intuition to bring greater power to your life. Entire books have been written on the subject,[11] but these tips will get you started:

- *Have a goal or question for your unconscious mind to work with.* Somewhere in my mind, I knew I wanted to be a writer. I also wanted a good part-time job during the school year.
  Give your unconscious mind a goal and let it work for

you. Or ask yourself a question: anything from "Where did I put that phone number?" to "Which project should I work on next?" Then let go. Stop thinking about it and do something else.

- *Get your conscious mind out of the way.* I got the idea to apply for the job while driving my car—when my mind was, if not in a meditative state, relaxed by the hum of the engine and the rhythmic action of shifting gears. Lots of people get intuitive insights in cars. Some people get them in the shower or while running, knitting, gardening, or performing some other repetitive activity.

- *Listen with discernment.* It's easy to tell intuition from rational deliberation. Intuition comes in a flash. The real trick is telling the difference between intuition and emotional impulse, since both arise spontaneously.

  The important difference, I've found, is in the emotional coloring. If you're really excited about some idea or action, then it's probably an emotional impulse. If, on the other hand, you feel a calm, centered, and deliberate inclination to do something, it's probably intuition. The final part of discernment is asking if this choice is a healthy one—for yourself and others. Our intuition does *not* ask us to commit harmful acts.

- *Follow your intuitive guidance and test the results.* If the proposed action is healthy and life-supporting, then follow through and see what happens. What new possibilities does your intuition bring?

You might want to keep an "intuition log," recording, at the end of each day, the insights that came your way, what you were doing at the time, how you felt, and what you discovered. As you learn to trust your intuition and follow your inner wisdom, you'll find yourself becoming more confident.

# 力 Pointers for Greater Power and Peace

*Cultivating the strengths of yin and yang and becoming comfortable with your own unique balance will increase your personal power.*

■ *Develop the strength of* yin *through greater mindfulness and self-acceptance.*

- Practice the strength of humility, recognizing what you do not know in order to keep learning.
- Become like water, overcoming resistance with the strength of perseverance.
- Extend the strength of compassion by actively listening to others.
- Honor your intuition: Follow your own inner wisdom.

■ *Develop the strength of* yang *by becoming more aware of your* ki, *your vital energy.*

- Avoid self-defeating, energy-draining habits.
- Develop a regular means of recharging your energy.
- Maintain a positive attitude.
- Nurture yourself regularly with healthy foods, exercise, and recreation.
- Practice *misogi* breathing.
- Remember to smile.

留心

# The Lesson of Agency

Treasure this knowledge:
The woman of Tao
Wears common clothing
And precious jade
Close to the heart.

*TAO, 70* [1]

*J*ade, for the ancient Chinese, was a most precious possession, as strong and beautiful as integrity. Worn to preserve health and good fortune, jade jewelry was passed down in families for generations.

Like precious jade, a sense of agency brings strength and beauty to our lives. Agency is the ability to act or exert power. With agency, we approach life actively, optimistically, living with the heartfelt conviction that our choices make a difference. When faced with challenge, change, or discontent, we ask ourselves the dynamic question "What can I do about it?" and answer with the power of our own creative action.

Mary Ann has always lived with a sense of agency. She grew up in the 1920s, when much of America retained the bloom of youthful optimism. The skies above her home in Pasadena, California, were still bright blue, the sunlight so intense the movie industry had set up their cameras in nearby Hollywood. Evening breezes were scented with orange blossoms from orchards stretching across the landscape. The area to the north that became California's Silicon Valley was covered with fruit trees and called the Valley of Heart's Delight.

Mary Ann's childhood was sheltered by a large, extended family, warmed by friendships, neighborhood softball games, and long summers at the beach. Carefree and confident, she whirled across the floor in her teens to the big band sound of Glenn Miller. I recall a picture of her at seventeen, dressed in shorts and holding a tennis racket. Her dark curls were brushed back from her face, her chin tilted up, and she met the camera with a direct gaze and relaxed smile. Athletic, optimistic, and naturally beautiful, she had a look of determination, open to life and ready for her own adventure.

The distant rumblings of a world at war brought an abrupt end to the golden youth of her generation. Mary Ann left Pasadena Junior College to work at a Lockheed assembly plant. The boys she'd known in school left to join the war in Europe and the Pacific. Some became combat pilots. Many of them died.

One day, as Mary Ann watched the planes come down the assembly line, she decided she could do more than build airplanes. She could fly them. She joined the Women's Air Force Service Pilots (WASP), an elite group of women pilots founded by Jacqueline Cochran to support the war effort. Packing up a few belongings, she left for basic training in Sweetwater, Texas.

The WASP went through the same training as male military pilots. They marched, did calisthenics, and stood for inspection. Mornings were marked by reveille before dawn and 7:00 A.M. training flights in an open cockpit Stearman. Being stretched to new limits was, for Mary Ann, both invigorating and empowering. Many others washed out.

Dressed in baggy flying suits made for men, Mary Ann and her classmates flew all kinds of military aircraft, including T6s, B17s, B29s, and P51 Mustangs. After graduation they were assigned to military bases around the country, flying cargo and transport and towing targets for gunnery practice.

These women shattered stereotypes left and right. One of Mary Ann's duties was to fly top military officers from one base to another. Told that his pilot would meet him on the flight line at 0800 hours, more than one self-important colonel did a double-take when he saw a young woman in her twenties dressed in flight gear standing by the plane. When a squadron of male pilots was reluctant to fly the formidable new B29, the commanding officer had two WASP land one at their base. When the men saw the women pilots emerge from the cockpit, their reluctance disappeared.

One of only 1,074 women among the many thousands of military pilots during World War II, Mary Ann flew with precision and confidence until the WASP were disbanded on December 20, 1944. There was no fanfare for these women pilots. The government did not even provide burial for those killed in the line of duty. It withheld the military benefits they'd been promised until an Act of Congress finally granted them, over thirty years late, in 1979. By then, since their discharge date was 1944, nearly all their benefits had expired. Yet the WASP demonstrated that women were capable and courageous, able to fly complex military aircraft. My mother, Mary Ann Dreher, and others like her led the way to a new definition of womanhood, characterized by active agency.

I grew up surrounded by photographs and stories of these brave women who flew so high above the rest. I've always been proud of my mother for flying those impressive planes, but above all for her indomitable spirit. As a military aviator, athlete, artist, and military wife, she repeatedly answered life's questions with her own dynamic response. With a sense of agency that made life an adventure, she led our family on excursions all over the world, packing up and moving from post to post. She taught me many things—lessons in history and geography, how to draw and paint, bake cakes, pack a suitcase, use a hammer, and reupholster furniture.

Like other daughters, I've gone through many relationships with my mother, looked up to her, idolized her, envied her, and disagreed with her. But most of all I've admired her—for showing me that women can reach for the sky and for living with agency, courage, and grace.[2]

## AFFIRMING AGENCY

WOMEN ARE not always reinforced for agency, for thinking, acting, and shaping their own lives. Such women are seen as threatening by people who cling to the old patriarchal patterns. For centuries, women were praised for putting their needs aside to care for others. But as Betty Friedan declared to a new generation of women in *The Feminine Mystique,* "there would be no sense in my writing this book at all if I did not believe that women can affect society, as well as be affected by it; that, in the end, a woman, as a man, has the power to choose, and to make her own heaven or hell."[3]

## WHY WOMEN ABDICATE AGENCY

Yet even today, many of us often shy away from living with agency, letting external circumstances make our choices for us. We do this for many reasons.

- *We've been conditioned to be passive.* At age ten, most young girls are curious and adventurous. They run and play, ask questions, and enjoy learning. But by early adolescence, they're told to "behave like young ladies," rein in their energies and cultivate the artificial manners and appearance deemed attractive by society and the media. Life, once embraced as an expansive adventure, now shrinks to a narrow concern with being popular, looking like a model, and having a boyfriend. Psychologist Emily Hancock urges all women to reclaim that "vital self first articulated in childhood, a root identity that gets cut off in the process of growing up female."[4]
- *It seems easier to be passive.* Surrendering to the pressures around us, we let others have their way because it seems easier to give in and because we are afraid of saying no, hurting people's feelings, and not being liked. Putting the power outside ourselves relieves us of responsibility. We're free to blame others rather than confront difficult issues or risk changing our lives. But what "seems" easier traps us in a position of powerlessness, unable to reach for our dreams.
- *We're too busy to make mindful choices.* Today's world con-

fronts women with a dizzying array of choices and commitments. We can become so busy that we merely react, surrendering personal responsibility to the pressures of time. To live with active agency, we must take charge, resist time's pressures, and make conscious choices.

Whether we realize it or not, actively or passively, we are always making choices. When we exercise agency, we choose actively, creatively shaping the pattern of our lives. Without agency, we surrender our choices to outside forces. Each of us is given her own set of circumstances, but ultimately, our success in life is determined by how we *meet* life's challenges. A sense of agency makes the difference between a life lived creatively or reactively, between a woman who makes things happen and one who complains that things are always happening to her.

## AGENCY AND OPTIMISM

STUDIES HAVE shown that it's not what happens around us but what happens *within* us that makes all the difference in our lives. Our "explanatory style,"[5] or how we explain our successes and failures to ourselves, informs our identity and worldview. By becoming more aware of your explanatory style, you can increase your sense of agency.

Every life has its ups and downs, but agents are optimists, who respond to life with confidence, claiming a pattern of success as their norm. They brush off failures as isolated events, but when something good happens they embrace it as part of their life's pattern in terms that are personal, permanent, and pervasive.[6] When Susan, an optimist, won a national poetry award, she said, "Yes, isn't it great [pervasive]? I had a feeling I'd win this year [personal]. I've put a lot of time into my writing lately and it's made a difference [permanent]."

Unsuccessful people affirm a sense of chronic incompetence—psychologist Martin Seligman calls this "learned helplessness."[7] Their reactions to the ups and downs of life are just the reverse. When something good happens to them, they find it hard to believe. "It was just luck," they say. But when something bad happens, they claim it as part of their life's pattern in terms that are personal, permanent, and pervasive. If Sara, a pessimist, tries a new recipe that flops, she says, "I'm a terrible cook" [personal]. "I'm *always* screwing up" [permanent]. "I can't do anything right" [pervasive]. Susan, the optimist, brushes it off, concluding, "It was obviously not a good recipe."

Champion athletes develop what Seligman calls "learned optimism."[8] When they falter, they barely skip a beat. Watching the 1997 women's world figure skating competition, I marveled at the balance, strength, and precision of these women. What impressed me most was how some of them could take a difficult jump, fall on the ice in front of thousands of people—and get up and keep on skating. They'd courageously continue with their routine, often taking that same jump again, this time successfully. They could not continue if they focused on failure.

Agents are powerful realists. They don't ignore mistakes but see them as part of their pattern of success. Instead of getting caught up in a negative spiral of self-doubt, professional athletes look at errors objectively, as information they can use to become more successful. After a competition, they ask themselves, "What can I learn from this?" "How can I do better next time?"

Like Kristi Yamaguchi, Michelle Kwan, Tara Lipinski, and others before them, champion figure skaters combine strength, precision, and grace with the discipline of learned optimism. In other arenas as well, the losers in life fixate on failure. Life's winners respond with agency and keep moving forward.

### BECOMING MINDFUL OF YOUR EXPLANATORY STYLE

The next time something *good* happens to you, watch your response. Are you an optimistic agent or a helpless victim? Which do you say?

"Thank you," acknowledging to yourself that you deserve it (optimistic agent), or

"I was just lucky, I guess" (helpless victim)

The next time you make a *mistake* or something breaks, watch your response. Which do you say?

"I'm such a klutz." "I've ruined it." "I can never do anything right" (helpless victim), or

"It broke. What can I do about it?" (optimistic agent)

By becoming more aware of your explanatory style and cultivating optimism, you can affirm greater agency and build a new momentum of success.

Optimism can even improve your health. Studies in the United States and Britain have revealed that people with a sense of agency stay healthier and live longer than those who feel like helpless victims. More influential than even socioeconomic status or access to health care, our attitude affects our daily lives in subtle but powerful ways.[9]

## COPING WITH CHANGE: AGENCY AS DYNAMIC GROWTH

THE *TAO TE CHING* reminds us that life is continuous movement:

*The movement of Tao*
*Is eternal return,*
*Gentleness*
*Its enduring strength.*
*Mother of ten thousand things,*
*It gives birth to being*
*From nonbeing.*
TAO, 40

Nothing in the universe stands still. Astronomers report new galaxies being born. Quantum mechanics reveals that the smallest building blocks of existence are neither particles nor waves but something in between. Nothing in our world is as solid as it appears. Everything from the new physics to the nightly news reminds us that the only constant in life is change.

Agency means accepting change as natural, realizing that the "status quo" is never static. Our lives, our bodies, our families, our relationships, and our world itself are always evolving. Instead of clinging to a past we cannot regain, living with agency means seeing new opportunities in every season of life. Research has shown that people who see change as natural are also less susceptible to illness than those who see change as a threat to their security.[10]

## RESISTANCE TO CHANGE

Change can energize us, but it also involves risk, as we leave behind familiar patterns. Often someone on a program of self-improvement will meet resistance from family and friends. "You've changed," they'll say accusingly. "That's not like you," trying to get her back into the old pattern.

One woman I know began a program of diet and exercise,

gradually losing fifty pounds. As the pounds melted away and she exchanged her old baggy clothes for stylish new outfits, many people tried to undermine her resolution. Friends invited her to indulge herself at lunch, saying to one another that they "liked the old Clara better." Her husband grew anxious and insecure, afraid that other men would find her more attractive and he might lose her.

Here she was, happier, healthier, and more energetic than she'd been in years, and the most important people in her life were blocking her progress. The change in her appearance upset their sense of security. They'd grown too comfortable with the heavier, less threatening Clara to celebrate her new sense of self.

## ACCEPTING CHANGE

Does this story strike a familiar chord? Has anyone told you "You've changed" lately with a tone of disapproval? Or have you felt threatened by a change in someone you know? If so, remind yourself, "I live in a dynamic universe." Then listen carefully to the fear of change in yourself or the other person. What is it telling you? How can you claim your security on a deeper level?

Quite often, one spouse is threatened when the other returns to school or begins anything new, from an exercise program to a career. Parents are often left with an empty feeling when their children leave home. Familiar patterns are broken and people feel lost, wondering where they fit now. At these times, it's important to listen compassionately to ourselves and others, looking beneath the changes to regain our faith in life.

## Finding Joy and Meaning in All the Seasons of Your Life

AS THE years move on, we witness many changes. We will see familiar people and places with the light of discernment, which illuminates the true and eliminates the false. We will overcome old habits that no longer serve us. Each season of life offers opportunities to exercise agency, to become more joyously and powerfully ourselves.

## The Season of Spring: Discovery and Self-Definition

WE EMERGE from childhood to young womanhood in the season of spring, which lasts from our early teens to mid-twenties. Our affirmation of agency in this crucial season involves discovery and self-definition. But this is when our commercial culture assaults girls with what psychologist Mary Pipher calls "junk values," an obsessive emphasis on appearance, sexuality, and submissive female roles that undermines their sense of self.[11] Advertising campaigns are designed to sell products, not promote healthy role models. In *Reviving Ophelia,* Pipher describes the ambushes that await adolescent girls. Those who avoid the dangers of drugs, school dropout, teenage pregnancy, and eating disorders are the ones who discard the "junk values" and define themselves with a sense of agency.[12]

### Helping Girls Develop Agency

Eileen Vierra works with SPEAK-UP! Leadership Program for Girls in San Jose, California. A dynamic young woman in her early thirties, she's committed to helping teenaged girls develop agency. SPEAK UP! was developed by a group called "20% plus by 2020," dedicated to increasing the number of women in corporate and political leadership to at least 20% by the year 2020. One way to do this, they realized, was to offer healthy values and role models to girls in early adolescence.

During the twelve-week SPEAK UP! course the girls meet women leaders in politics, science, and the arts, learning to see women—and ultimately themselves—as active agents. They attend workshops on personal finance, communication, and negotiation, participate in group activities, and improve their communication skills by giving speeches on videotape. Using her background in finance and counseling psychology, Eileen helps the girls identify leadership qualities in themselves and recognize that agency is an ongoing journey of self-discovery and active choice.[13]

## DISCOVERING YOUR DEFINING MOMENT

WE OFTEN experience agency in *defining moments,* situations in early life that help us discover who we are. A defining moment can be a personal victory, an accomplishment— your first piano recital, winning a race, overcoming an obstacle. Sometimes a defining moment comes when you least expect it. Sometimes it comes from breaking the rules.

At seventeen, I was a high school senior, quiet, studious, and a member of the National Honor Society. Girls with good grades at Kaiserslautern American High School in Germany were given the dubious honor of working in the school office instead of sitting through study hall. I'd take pink requisition slips and call other students in to see the principal for disciplinary action. Often, this meant calling Mike Carney out of

Miss Ackerman's second period English class. Mike was always breaking the rules—leaving campus for lunch, asking impertinent questions, joking in class, wearing his shirttail out. The principal had his eagle eye out for Mike. In the school hierarchy, I was an honor student and Mike was a troublemaker. But I liked Mike. His outrageous questions and ever-present sense of fun tormented the teachers and made even the dullest class enjoyable.

Like everyone, I knew that Mike and Cindi were a couple. She took the bus in from Ramstein Air Force Base like me, while Mike commuted by train from Pirmasens Army Barracks. Mike and Cindi saw each other at school, but going on dates was much more complicated.

One Thursday morning in April, the world was suddenly spring. As I walked into the principal's office, the sun was streaming through the windows and the trees outside were covered with white blossoms. But there in the office sat Cindi, clutching her books to her chest, her eyes red and swollen.

Mrs. Winters, the school secretary, told me my assignment was to help Cindi check herself and her brothers out of school. Her brothers were home with the measles and the whole family was being air evacuated back to the States the next day because Cindi's mother had cancer. I was to help clean out their lockers and check in their books and supplies. Her father would be back to pick her up in the afternoon. After I mumbled an awkward, "I'm sorry," we walked down the dark hallway in silence to Cindi's locker, cleaned it out, and returned all her books.

On the way to her brothers' lockers, we passed Miss Ackerman's second period class. I paused before the door, realizing what I could do and knowing it was against all the rules.

Then, without any authorization, I stepped inside and

walked to the front of the class, saying, as normally as possible, "Will Mike Carney please come to the office?" Miss Ackerman never asked to see the pink slip. She barely looked up from her desk.

It didn't take much explanation when Mike joined us in the hall. "I'm supposed to help Cindi check out of school, but I think she needs your help more than mine," I said. He put his arm around her and they walked down the long empty hallway together, to pack up and say good-bye.

Mike never went back to class that day. They checked in all the books and then spent the rest of the day together until Cindi's father arrived at three. I went home feeling a heavy mixture of sadness, seriousness, and foreboding. The next morning, the principal called me into his office.

"This is a very serious offense," he said, with a stern look on his face. "You could be expelled from school."

Feeling strangely detached, I looked out the window at the white blossoms against the clear blue sky.

"We could call in your parents," he continued. "You could never receive your high school diploma."

I looked back at him. I'd already received my acceptance to UCLA.

"Do you know what you did was wrong?" he asked.

I looked down and said nothing, feeling that what I'd done wasn't wrong at all.

"Do you realize that you broke the rules?" he asked impatiently.

"Yes," I said in a low voice, feeling almost numb.

"Can you promise this will never happen again?" he asked, looking down at me through his horn-rimmed glasses.

How could it? "Yes," I said. "This situation will never happen again."

"Then we will forgive your offense this time," he said, "based upon your academic record. But if anything like this ever happens again, you'll be expelled from school."

I left the office for the study hall, where I spent second period until the end of the year.

The principal expected me to feel guilty. Perhaps I did, for I never told my parents. But I walked out of his office that day with a new sense of freedom. I'd always tried so hard to do the right thing; now I'd broken the rules and survived. I knew in my heart that giving Mike and Cindi a chance to say good-bye was worth the risk, that there was a difference between the inflexible rules of this principal and the deeper principle I'd chosen. Years later, I still value in myself that shy, studious girl who was brave enough to break the rules in order to follow her heart.

We all have such defining moments when we develop greater agency by reaching out and discovering who we are in small acts of courage. Looking back on the springtime of your life, what is one moment you're proud of? What does it tell you about who you are and what you value? Can you apply this lesson to the way you live today?

## THE SEASON OF SUMMER: CHALLENGE AND CREATIVITY

LIFE'S SECOND stage, the season of summer, takes us from our late twenties into our thirties and early forties, bringing us into the fullness of life with all its complications. We affirm agency in this busy season by exercising our creativity, shaping our lives into patterns of joy and meaning. The season of summer calls on every woman to become the artist of her own life.

This personal artistry can be a creative response to life's challenges or assembling the materials of your life into a collage of beauty and value. My friend Sherry, who spent this season of life at home with her two small children, believes that "creativity is more than producing a product or 'work of art.'" It is a state of mind, the ability to respond thoughtfully, even playfully, to the opportunities around us, to find meaningful self-expression in the commonplace. Sherry says she found herself becoming highly creative on rainy days in a small house with two young children, responding to their need for activity with the materials she had on hand. Baking cookies together, telling stories, playing games, listening to the rain can be done halfheartedly or with the sense of joy and celebration that makes them creative affirmations.[14]

Psychologist Abraham Maslow identified creativity as essential to a life of self-actualization. One woman's creative response to daily life made him expand his definition. As he explained, "One woman, uneducated, poor, a full-time housewife and mother, did none of these conventionally creative things, and yet was a marvelous cook, mother, wife, and homemaker. With little money, her home was somehow always beautiful. She was a perfect hostess. Her meals were banquets. Her taste in linens, silver, glass, crockery, and furniture was impeccable. She was in all these areas original, novel, ingenious, unexpected, inventive. I just *had* to call her creative. I learned from her and others like her that a first-rate soup is more creative than a second-rate painting, and that, generally, cooking or parenthood or making a home could be creative while poetry need not be."[15] It is not our circumstances or materials but our *response* to them that makes us creative, as we exercise agency in the art of living.

# *T*HE SEASON OF AUTUMN: RECOGNITION AND HARVEST

THE SEASON of autumn takes us into our forties and fifties, bringing harvest and recognition. We exercise agency in this period by creatively coping with change in everything from our life patterns to our own bodies. This is the time when our careers bear fruit, when we reap accomplishments and rewards. In this season, Bella Abzug was elected to Congress, Johnetta Cole became president of Spelman College, cardiologist Helen Taussig developed an operation to save the lives of "blue babies," and Karen Blixen wrote *Out of Africa*. Carolyn Heilbrun said that for her, fifty had been "a time of flowering," that "women seldom think of themselves in their prime at fifty, but I think it is often so."[16]

Autumn is the season when our children grow up and leave home, forcing us to make adjustments in life's familiar patterns. Some women deal with this change better than others. Many cling to the past, leaving their children's rooms unchanged for years. Others transform that space into a guest room, home office, or hobby room. This is symbolic of turning from an emphasis on our families and the others in our lives to a renewed emphasis on ourselves.

In autumn, we enter what Gail Sheehy has called the "silent passage" of menopause. What this passage means is different for every woman. Some women fight it, others mourn; Margaret Mead embraced it as a threshold to "postmenopausal zest." After menopause, our bodies can no longer bear children, but we can exercise our creative power in other ways. Some women begin new careers. Gail Sheehy described this time as exhilarating for many women who leave old patterns of accommodation behind and are finally free to be themselves.[17]

Some women still deny their age. When a news story about me appeared a while ago, noting my age as forty-nine, a woman colleague asked if I minded that the article mentioned my age. "Why should I?" I answered. "It's a fact." The year Gloria Steinem celebrated her fiftieth birthday and people told her she didn't look fifty, she responded, "This is how fifty looks." The *Tao* reminds us to transcend limited definitions of age and beauty, recognizing that:

> *When some are called beautiful*
> *The rest are seen as ugly.*
> *When we prize one quality as good,*
> *The rest become inferior.*
>
> *Yet each extreme complements the other.*
> *Large and small,*
> *Light and dark,*
> *Short and tall,*
> *Youth and age*
> *Bring balance to life.*
> TAO, 2

Following the Tao, we learn to see beauty in every season of life.

## *I*NDIAN SUMMER: NEW BEGINNINGS AND TERRA INCOGNITA

WITH AUTUMN comes Indian summer, which the Chinese call the fifth season, a time of new beginnings for many women. This season remains for many people terra incognita, the term Renaissance map makers gave to uncharted territory. Gail Sheehy, who "couldn't envision anything past fifty" when she wrote *Passages*, has begun to chart this territory in *New Passages*. Sheehy believes that our increased life span has given us the gift of "second adulthood," a new span of life to explore, a time for new dreams and new beginnings.[18]

With her copper-colored hair, amber jewelry, and spirit of adventure, Peggy personifies for me this vibrant season. A pathfinder in terra incognita, she went back to school after marriage and children, earning her Ph.D. in political science at age fifty-three. With the conventional career path blocked because of her age, she accepted a part-time teaching position at Santa Clara University. I remember walking past her classroom one day, wondering who this remarkable woman was, whose charisma reminded me of Margaret Mead and the Kennedys, people who pursued life with a passion and passed it on to others in empowering ways.

In 1991, Peggy and three women friends put together a national conference at Esalen Institute on "The New Older Woman." They asked themselves what they, as women over fifty, wanted to do with their lives and decided to ask that question of other "new older women" in our society. They had no grants, no financial backing, no stipends, only an idea: a dynamic dialogue for women of achievement over fifty. Esalen liked the idea and sponsored its first workshop exclusively for women. The participants were an impressive collection of architects, writers, artists, scientists, women such as Mary Catherine Bateson, Gail Sheehy, Claire Falkenstein, and others who had made major contributions to their fields. Peggy and her friends then wrote a book, *The New Older Woman: A Dialogue for the Coming Century*, showing how women can exercise agency in the second half of life.

Several years ago, Peggy's husband, Chuck, was diagnosed with cancer. For years, he fought to recover and they bravely captured what joy they could, celebrating life together through the struggle and writing a book, *Dialogue of Hope: Talking Our Way Through Cancer*.[19] After Chuck died, Peggy's friends introduced her to a man who had lost his wife of many years, also to cancer, recommending that he read her book. In time, that man became her husband, ushering in a new chapter in her life. When I last saw her, she told me she had just celebrated her sixty-seventh birthday with her new husband, Jack, riding a zodiac and watching whales in the Gulf of Mexico. As always, celebrating life, she was ready for her next adventure.[20]

Indian summer is an unexpected season, a bright and beautiful gift often occurring in the midst of challenge and loss. Like the Chinese character for "crisis," which contains the two characters of "danger" and "opportunity," within many challenging situations there is an Indian summer, a sudden gift of joy, if we can follow our hearts and live with agency.

## $\mathcal{T}$HE SEASON OF WINTER: SERENITY, SIMPLICITY, AND STEWARDSHIP

WITH THE increased life span of current generations, it's hard to discern just when the shift occurs into the serenity of life's final season. Some women remain professionally active in their seventies and eighties. Others narrow their lives in their sixties. As we enter the stage of life Erik Erikson called "Integrity," the season of winter brings us more deeply into terra incognita. There are few markers and guidelines. Anthropologist Mary Catherine Bateson has said, "To be in your seventies now is to embark on a truly uncharted sea. Growing up we had so few to point the way, to pass on what was possible for older women."[21]

## THE QUEST FOR SIMPLICITY

In the season of winter we need to simplify, eliminating the nonessential in order to focus, in the time that remains, upon what we truly value. When my friend Genevieve entered her seventies, she and her husband sold their home and moved into a new condominium that would require less upkeep than their acre of mountain property. She also began giving things away, consciously shedding and simplifying. I have a beautiful lamp of hers in my bedroom and some of her books in my study. Another friend, Elizabeth, moved herself into a retirement center with organized activities, an evening meal, and health care for those who needed it. Both women are still active and healthy. But they wanted to provide for their comfort and security, to enjoy this season of life, and not risk becoming dependent on their families, still in the busy summer of their lives.[22]

In the season of winter, wise women exercise agency, consciously choosing the shape of their lives, while their reactive sisters face this season in frantic denial. One extreme example is just down the street from me, the Winchester Mystery House in San Jose, California. Sarah Winchester felt that as long as her house was under construction she could postpone the inevitable. She spent much of the Winchester rifle fortune to engage workmen in continuous activity, building a house with 160 rooms, secret passageways, halls that lead nowhere, and stairways that reach up to the ceiling. Few women go to the extreme of Sarah Winchester, but continuous agitation is *not* the way of wisdom. Filling their calendars, their closets, their lives with clutter, commotion, and collectibles, too many women deny themselves the space of contemplation.

## SERENITY AND GOOD STEWARDSHIP

Ideally, as our lives shift into the season of winter, we will become the equivalent of village elders, wise women who share their wisdom with others. One example of this is my friend Gertrude, who, after an active life working and raising two daughters, chose to spend this season affirming her most cherished beliefs.

Whether volunteering at homeless shelters, participating in demonstrations, speaking with the city council, or teaching nonviolence classes for her church, Gertrude brings an affirmation of peace wherever she goes. With her bright blue eyes and radiant smile, she reaches out with consideration to everyone she meets—political leaders, homeless people, and those who disagree with her. She listens with respect to them all, dissolving barriers and living the peace she believes in.

I see her as a beautiful example of a woman who lives the Tao. She begins each day with prayer, which centers and sustains her. Moving through her work with a sense of flow, she maintains her faith in the process, even when there are no immediate results. As chair of the social action and education committee for the county council of churches, she works to set up temporary shelters for the homeless in nearby places of worship, providing education and job placement to help them build better lives. Practicing other strengths of Tao, Gertrude simplifies her life to focus on what matters most. Mindful of her timing, aware of the energies within and around her, she knows when to move forward on a project, when to wait. Courageous enough to speak up for her beliefs, compassionate enough to listen, she blends the strengths of *yin* and *yang*. Balancing her active commitment to social justice with quiet time with her husband at the end of the day, she lives her life with the power of agency, following the path with heart.

Her example has become an inspiration to her community. In 1992, the Santa Clara Council of Churches established the Gertrude Welch Ecumenical Award in her honor. This award is given annually to an individual whose life and work advance the cause of peace and justice.[23]

## *M*ENTORS AND ROLE MODELS

IN THE season of winter, many women's household duties are reduced, giving them more time to share their wisdom with the larger community. Listening mindfully, telling their stories, affirming the value of the people they meet in ways our busy society often neglects, wise women are a valuable resource for us all. Some become mentors for younger women, sharing their wisdom and expertise, supporting a new generation in reaching for their dreams.

Each woman has her own role models who show us what women can be. Along with many others, I owe a debt to Louisa May Alcott and admired Jo in *Little Women* for her brave and independent spirit. I have pictures of Eleanor Roosevelt in both my office at school and my study at home, having "adopted" her as an example of a woman who transcended herself, her personal obstacles, and her time, leaving a legacy of hope for those who come after her. I admire Helen Nearing, who with her husband, Scott, built their stone house by hand and mindfully created the structure of their lives in eloquent simplicity and dedication to their beliefs.

Two other role models are anthropologist Margaret Mead and ethologist Jane Goodall, who charted new patterns in their lives and work.

But such examples are barely enough to light up the dim archetype of the wise woman of the village when our culture needs a bright and shining star. At "The New Older Woman" conference described earlier, clinical psychologist Dr. Eleanor Zuckerman said, "Our society doesn't have any wise, mature position for us to move on to, there's nothing defined and ready for us, and that's why we have to make it for ourselves—change the playing field, make our own new definition."[24]

## AFFIRMING AGENCY IN ALL THE SEASONS

OUR SITUATIONS shift with the seasons, but our task in the season of winter is fundamentally the same as in the first season of our lives and every season thereafter: to affirm our own identity and live with a spirit of agency, actively choosing the shape of our lives. In so doing, we discover joy and meaning in every season and leave a shining legacy of what it means to be a woman.

## *Pointers for Greater Power and Peace*

*Whatever your season of life—spring, summer, autumn, or winter—these practices will increase your sense of agency.*

■ *Ask yourself the dynamic question: "What can I do about it?"*

Whenever you face challenge, disappointment, or your own discontent in any area of life, don't just sit there feeling unhappy.

- Ask yourself, "What can I do about it?"
- Brainstorm. Write down some actions you can take.
- Choose one and take that action.

The important thing is not to get stuck in passivity but to take positive action. Agents act and make a difference in their lives. Nonagents only worry and complain—about everything from their hair to their careers and relationships. Remember to ask the dynamic question and affirm your own power to act.

■ *Develop learned optimism.*[25]

- Become more aware of your explanatory style and modify it to strengthen your sense of agency.
- The next time something *good* happens, claim success as your life's pattern in ways that are personal, permanent, and pervasive. Tell yourself, "I did it. I worked hard to accomplish this. I'm a winner."
- The next time you meet with *disappointment,* external-

ize and isolate the negative event and then move on. Tell yourself, "The _____ [fill in the blank] broke down. This is an isolated incident. I'm moving on to greater success."

■ *Begin a mentoring relationship with another woman.*

- Whatever season of life you're in now, you can increase your wisdom and personal power through the process of mentoring.
- If you are just entering a profession, find a woman in your field who has done something you admire. Invite her to lunch and ask her how she did it. Apply some of her lessons to your life.
- If you are in the season of autumn or winter, find a young woman and meet with her, asking about her dreams and goals. Listen, offer moral support, and learn your own lessons from the process.
- Whether you are officially the "mentor" or "mentee," mentoring becomes a circular relationship of listening, sharing, and mutual empowerment. *Both* people give and receive, creating more together than either could alone.

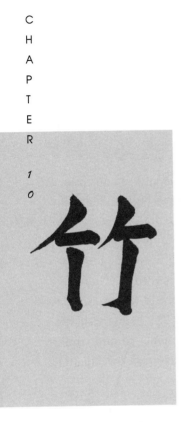

# The Lesson of Harmony

Follow *wu wei*.
Act without effort.
Watch the patterns,
Large and small,
Transcending conflict
With character.

*T A O .  6 3*

For centuries, Chinese painters and calligraphers have learned their art by painting bamboo. With its slender stalks and delicate leaves, it looks like a piece of calligraphy itself. Bamboo has inspired poets and artists with its perfect balance of *yin* and *yang*, strength and flexibility. Standing straight and tall, its graceful stalks swaying in the wind, bamboo bends but does not break. When the wind passes, it returns to its upright position, a model of integrity.

A symbol of endurance and aspiration, bamboo is evergreen and long-lasting, rising up to one hundred feet. Its hollow core is like the contemplative center of our lives. In the Far East, its gifts extend to hundreds of daily uses. Bamboo provides shade and shelter in gardens. Its stems are made into tools, cooking utensils, and brushes for painting and calligraphy. Its pulp becomes paper; its stalks, fuel; its leaves, thatched roofs. Bamboo shoots are eaten as vegetables, its seeds and roots used for medicine. The strong and resilient trunks become furniture or scaffolding to build modern skyscrapers.

Affirming flexibility and resourcefulness, wise women create harmony in their lives with the strength of bamboo. They see into the natural order of things with the "detached, Taoist, passive, non-interfering awareness" Abraham Maslow equated with self-actualization.[1] To bend with life's storms and never break, to reframe challenge and conflict into new patterns of harmony is the lesson of this chapter.

## €MBRACING THE TIGER: RESOLVING CONFLICT

THERE'S A posture in tai ch'i called "embrace tiger and return to mountain." Many women are about as comfortable facing conflict as they'd be embracing a tiger. Psychiatrist Jean Baker Miller says, "Conflict has been a taboo area for women and for key reasons. Women were supposed to be the quintessential accommodators, mediators, the adapters, and soothers."[2] When we experience conflict, we think something is wrong with *us*, that it's our fault. For years, whenever anything went wrong, I'd say, "I'm sorry," even if I hadn't caused the problem. Do you do this too?

For centuries, women were conditioned to develop the strength of *yin*—to be open, receptive, and nurturing. We were the primary caregivers for our children, creating homes of comfort and security, preparing food, and nurturing life in countless ways. Busy meeting others' needs, we often brushed our own aside. When conflict occurred, it seemed our responsibility to sweep it up as we would a broken dish, arranging the pieces of our lives into more accommodating patterns.

Even today, as women exercise agency in our professional lives, becoming architects, artists, and astronauts, too many of us still shrink in the face of conflict. Psychologist Emily Hancock has noted that "females still grow up with the expectation that they will put aside their own needs in favor of tending to the personal comfort of those who surround them *simply because they are women.*"[3] When others are uncomfortable, we feel it's our fault or at least our responsibility and modify our actions to meet their needs.

Yet life is a dynamic balance of *yin* and *yang*. We cannot be fully ourselves if we are always receptive, always accommodating, always *yin*. And if we cannot be fully ourselves, how can others truly know us?

## A LESSON FROM AIKIDO

Aikido gives us an important lesson in reframing conflict. The word itself means "the way of harmonizing energy" (in Japanese, *ai* means "harmony," *ki* means "energy," and *do*, like *tao* in Chinese, means "the way"). Helping break down old habits of accommodation, aikido demonstrates that conflict is simply a matter of opposing energies. In most interpersonal conflicts, one person is not automatically "good," the other "bad." At that moment, their energies conflict.

They're going in different directions. Aikido works by acknowledging these energies and working with them, defusing an attack without harming the attacker.

I saw an example of aikido's power to redirect energies during my friend Kristie's black belt test. The mother of three young children, Kristie was one of the first people I met at the Fremont dojo. Small-boned and petite, as delicate as an orchid from her home in Vietnam, she stands five feet two in high heels, but her generous spirit and expansive energies are boundless.

At the black belt tests in San Jose, Kristie bowed onto the mat before rows of spectators and moved through the first part of her test with the grace of a ballerina. Her long black ponytail swirling behind her, she demonstrated one technique after another with a young Asian man as her partner.

Then the panel of judges asked her to demonstrate a technique called *irimi nage* with a fellow known as Big Mike. Mike lunged toward her with a clenched fist. Remaining centered, Kristie responded with the strength of bamboo. She stepped aside to avoid the blow, turned to blend with his energies in a graceful spiral, and finally threw him down with the force of his own attack. As Mike hit the mat with a resounding thud, it was obvious that Kristie had earned her black belt.[4]

Physically, aikido can be exhilarating. With the power of her own *ki*, a 100-pound woman can throw a 250-pound man. But aikido's psychological lessons are even more powerful, underscoring how we can respond to any conflict by remaining centered, working with the energies within and around us.

# THE *AIKI* WAY: TWO REACTIONS TO TRANSCEND

APPLYING THIS aikido lesson to our daily lives, we can re-define conflict as opposing energies. This new perspective liberates us from two habits that drain our energy, make us feel "wrong," and trap us in an attitude of helplessness. The first habit is catastrophizing; the second is polarizing.

## CATASTROPHIZING

EFFECTIVE CONFLICT resolution involves taking responsibility, but there's such a thing as taking *too much* responsibility. We catastrophize when we personalize and magnify conflict, blowing a problem out of proportion. I remember an incident from childhood that set me up for a long habit of catastrophizing.

When I was five years old, the red-glass candy dish in the living room was a family treasure. I would take out one of the chocolate kisses kept inside and peel away the silver foil. As the chocolate slowly melted in my mouth, I'd watch the afternoon sunlight glitter through the glass, shining on the wall in ruby red and rainbow patterns.

One day I reached up to get a piece of chocolate when suddenly the candy dish crashed to the floor, shattering into tiny fragments. I looked down in dismay. The beautiful dish was destroyed and I had done it. My mother rushed into the room. "Now I can't go to college," I cried in a fit of guilt and anguish.

My parents were, of course, upset. But they bought another candy dish and laughed for years about what I'd said. With the logic of a child, I'd connected their comments about "saving money for college" with the cost of replacing what seemed to me a priceless object. Having done this terrible thing, I obviously felt I did not deserve to go to college—whatever college meant to a five-year-old child.

At times, when things go wrong, I still catastrophize. Last spring when my computer got a virus, I felt horrible, convinced that the computer was destroyed, my writing project was ruined, and the virus was all my fault—when none of this was true. The next day, when I could see the problem more objectively, I talked to some people and got an antivirus program that cleared up the whole thing.

### CURES FOR CATASTROPHIZING

The next time something goes wrong, stop catastrophizing and ask yourself:

- What's *really* happening? (I don't mean how you feel about it. I mean *really* happening, as if you were writing a science report)
- Now, break the problem down into manageable steps.
- What can you do first?
- If you don't know what to do, who can you ask?
- If this person doesn't know, who else can you ask?
- What can you do then?
- Make a list of action steps—write them down.
- Take the first step.

Catastrophizing makes us feel awful—guilty, weak, helpless, and hopeless. The cure for catastrophizing is to see things more objectively. Telling someone else can help put a problem into perspective. The next step is to make a plan and work your plan. Affirm competence. Keep moving forward. As the *Tao* tells us:

*The Tao woman*
*Is not overwhelmed*
*By challenges.*
*She sees*
*The smaller steps*
*Within them.*
TAO, 63

## Polarizing

ANOTHER DESTRUCTIVE habit is polarizing. One of the underlying mind-sets of Western civilization, it makes us see differences as irreconcilable opposites. Becoming fixated on opposition, we cannot find harmony. Eastern philosophy offers a holistic vision that transcends polarization:

*In the beginning was the Tao*
*Which gave rise to* yin *and* yang,
*Sunlight and shadow,*
*And the energy*
*Of all existence.*
*Yet beneath the dance of life,*
*The Tao is always One,*
*Mother of ten thousand things,*
*Source of all creation.*
TAO, 42

The polarities of *yin* and *yang* originally meant only the shady and sunny sides of the same mountain, two parts of the same whole. Yet our Western minds too often polarize opposites, reducing them to either/or, right or wrong, us or them, all or nothing. This misperception is responsible for centuries of misunderstanding, turning conflict into combat.

The wisdom of Tao expands our perspective, showing us that life is not linear but circular. The familiar Taoist symbol of *Tai Ji* unites the contrasting forces of *yin* and *yang* into complementary harmony. A dark fish swims alongside a light fish in a circular embrace, each beginning where the other ends.

In nature, complementary opposition informs all of life. It is night and day, earth and sky, left and right, active and contemplative, self and other, and thousands of other polarities. One intimate example is the air we breathe. The trees around us breathe in what we breathe out, exchanging carbon dioxide for oxygen in an ongoing cycle that sustains the life on this planet.

### Looking Beyond Polarities

Just seeing polarities as complementary opposites will help you reconcile many conflicts. Do you know people whose habits annoy you? They are *yin* to your *yang*. Asking yourself why they upset you will move your energy out of opposition, giving you deeper insight into your values.

With insight comes greater understanding, less narrow-mindedness and separation. We all have our preferences. Some of us value privacy, resent interruptions, and prefer a carefully planned life. Others are more extroverted, dramatic, and spontaneous. I know one woman who took a year to plan her wedding and another who arranged hers in two days. The world is filled with contrasts. Mountains and valleys, *yang* and *yin,* are part of the landscape of life.

The polarities of *yin* and *yang* also occur within us. Some women feel they have to choose between family and career, personal and professional fulfillment, all or nothing, either/or. Or we let differences become barriers. Too many women divide up into camps of working mothers, stay-at-home mothers, or single women, with members of each group resenting the others instead of embracing one another as sisters who have taken different paths.

In recent history, the polarities of womanhood have taken many forms. In *The Feminine Mystique*, Betty Friedan wrote of the despair of many 1950s housewives who subordinated their needs to their families. The women's movement in the 1970s raised our consciousness as women but often divided us into opposing groups. The 1980s told us that we could "have it all," and many women combined families and fast-track careers, with life taking on a frantic pace.

More and more, we are realizing that fulfillment comes not from one extreme or the other or even from trying to do everything at once. It comes, instead, from finding your own pattern. What is right for one woman may not work for you or me.

The wisdom of Tao reminds us to honor our energies and those around us, to find our own path and walk it in joy, combining *yin* and *yang*, public and private, into new harmonies.

## *R*ESOLVING CONFLICTS WITH SHARED NEEDS

WHILE POLARIZATION gets people stuck in opposition, searching for shared needs can help us discover solutions.

"The Conflict Partnership Process" developed by my friend Dudley Weeks works with conflicts on all levels from the interpersonal to the international. Dudley is an international conflict-resolution facilitator and author of *The Eight Essential Steps to Conflict Resolution*. Like aikido, the heart of Dudley's process requires us to become more mindful of the energies within and around us, as we shift from demands, which divide us, to needs that unite us as partners in resolution.[5]

When people get caught up in demands, we become polarized, seeing only two possibilities—yours or mine—ignoring alternatives. Consider what would happen if we were cooking dinner together and both reached for the last lemon in the kitchen. I could respond with accommodation, letting you have the lemon, and my recipe would fall short. Or vice versa. Or we could compromise, each getting half a lemon. Each recipe would be less than what it could be.

When we act from the level of demands, those are our choices. But when we share our needs, we discover new possibilities. I am cooking fish and you're making lemon poppy seed muffins. I need only the lemon juice and you need only the lemon zest. So, after washing and grating off the peel, you hand the lemon to me to use in my recipe. That's harmony.

Of course, not all conflicts are this simple. But working from shared needs helps us move from polarization to new possibilities. In the summer of 1995, I interviewed Dudley Weeks in Washington, D.C., for my book on leadership. Impressed with the conflict partnership process, I wanted to take one of his workshops. But Dudley is based on the East Coast and I live in California. I wondered just how I could do it.

One day, the answer arrived at my door. Three women students came to see me because they'd studied with Dudley during a semester exchange in Washington and wanted to set up a conflict resolution program at our college. My need to take a workshop and their need to set up a program came together as a shared need. Together, we wrote a successful grant proposal, bringing Dudley out for a campus-wide presentation and workshop. More than two grants and two years later, dozens of people have learned the conflict partnership skills and shared them in their dormitories, offices, homes, and communities. In the spring of 1996, workshop participants honored the three women students who had founded the conflict resolution program as their graduation gift to the university.

Shared needs. We all got what we needed—and more. In conflict resolution as in the natural world, the whole is much more than the sum of its parts.

## Honoring Your Needs

THE FIRST lesson our workshops teach is that conflict is natural. Whenever two individuals or two groups come together for any length of time, differences arise.

Yet many women are uncomfortable dealing with conflict, so they become conflict avoiders, giving in to the other person, repressing their needs, hoping the conflict will go away. But conflict avoidance rarely works, especially in an ongoing relationship. There's more than a conflict hidden beneath the surface. There are buried resentment and frustration, which emerge in unexpected ways, creating friction and misunderstanding between ourselves and the other person.

Some women are so used to accommodating that conflict makes them feel numb. They can't even identify their own needs and feelings. Creative conflict resolution requires compassion—for ourselves as well as others. One Chinese character for compassion, *t'zu,* is made up of the character for abundant vegetation above the character for heart. Compassion means cultivating our own heart's garden, honoring our feelings, asking what we need in this situation.

The next time you find yourself in conflict, take time to listen to your heart, to ask what you really need. This may mean taking some time by yourself before meeting with the other person. When you have a clearer sense of what you need, you'll be more centered, more able to understand the other person.

### BUILDING BRIDGES TO RESOLUTION

Like any skill, conflict resolution takes practice. We have to get beyond either denying our feelings or blaming someone else. Learning to resolve conflicts, large and small, will bring greater power and peace to your life. You can begin building your own bridge to resolution by following the steps at the end of this chapter.

### YIN SKILLS AS YOUR NATURAL RESOURCE

IN CONFLICT resolution and other areas, our *yin* skills are valuable resources. Traditional "feminine" qualities—strong interpersonal skills, listening, nurturing, and caring—need *not* trap us in second-class, subservient roles. It is not the skills themselves that limit us, but the structures we've expressed them in. Actually, a greater concern for human values and relationships is exactly what our fast-paced, materialistic culture needs to become more balanced and more whole.

By using our *yin* skills to advantage rather than letting others use us, we can create new possibilities for ourselves and our world. University of California management professor Dr. Judy Rosener claims that most women possess the very leadership qualities our society needs in this era of change and uncertainty. The ability to handle many tasks at once, deal with ambiguity, cope with interruptions, build consensus, and communicate—the skills that make women good mothers, nurses, and teachers also make them good managers. In her research for the *Harvard Business Review* and for her book, *America's Competitive Secret: Utilizing Women as a Management Strategy,* Rosener says that women are our country's largest untapped resource. We possess the skills of "transformational leadership" vital to success in an increasingly complex, global, and rapidly changing world.[6]

## CREATING NEW HARMONIES

COMBINING THE courage of *yang* with the strength of *yin,* we can give ourselves, one another, and our world the gift of greater harmony. It is not the public achievements, the grand gestures, that make the greatest difference in our lives but the small choices we make each day. Our daily disciplines and discoveries transform life into a spiritual exercise, an ongoing journey of depth and meaning. The results of such mindful living are as beautiful and varied as the faces of women today.

By working to eliminate *mindless habits* and planting the seeds of *mindful practice,* we can cultivate lives of greater harmony.

## CREATING HARMONY AT HOME

ONE MINDLESS habit for many people is excessive television watching. It robs us of our time—the average American watches TV four to six hours a day—and reduces our days to programmed passivity. TV programs can give us useful information and recreation. But passive watching is no substitute for authentic living, whether that means taking time to be alone with your thoughts, listen to another person, enjoy a well-cooked meal, or reflect upon the beauty of a sunset or the light in a loved one's eyes.

Many women are eliminating this mindless habit. Annette, an insurance company manager, has set a margin of one hour before her daughter's bedtime when the TV is turned off. She and her husband use this time to read stories to their five-year-old daughter, relax, and center down for a good night's rest, without media noise and negative news droning in their ears.

Jill, a teacher, and her architect husband have gone a step further, making a conscious choice not to have television in their house. Jill spends time with her children, Aaron, eleven, and Hannah, eight, listening to music, reading, and working on art projects. Her children read to each other and both of them like to exercise their imagination making things. Hannah does embroidery and sews doll clothes. Like his father, Aaron likes to build things. He makes doll furniture for his sister and built a tree house in their backyard. Both enjoy science projects, art, and origami. Hannah and Aaron are bright, creative young people with original thoughts and questions, free from the daily programming of popular culture.[7]

Replacing mindless habits with mindful practice can make your life more harmonious. Religious communities have always structured their lives around ritual, with times for work, meals, and devotions. When I visited my friend Ann, a Holy Cross sister in Merrill, Wisconsin, I remember awakening to the sisters' singing in the chapel and watching them move through their days in patterns of order and grace. After morning mass and breakfast, some went off to their jobs as teachers, nurses, or social workers. Others worked in the convent. At the end of the day they gathered to give thanks and share their evening meal.

There's something sacred about breaking bread together, a celebration of life and community, although we don't always see it. When I was growing up, my family had dinner together every night at six. I remember my frustration at having to cut short my afternoon activities to get home in time for dinner.

"Why can't I just eat later?" I'd ask, annoyed at this restrictive routine.

"This is the only time we see each other all day," my mother would answer. With our varied schedules—work, school, chores, and social activities—dinner was the one time we gathered together as a family. Each night, my brother and I would be asked, "What did you learn in school today?" followed by more questions and discussion.

Many families today no longer have dinner together. They're so busy, they've replaced the evening meal with do-it-yourself "grazing." Instead of waiting for dinner, a hungry person goes out to the kitchen, pops a frozen dinner into the microwave, and eats, often in front of the TV set. Efficiency has replaced community.

Now I find myself enjoying the same ritual I once found so restrictive as a child. Every night, my husband and I take turns cooking dinner. I enjoy the *yin* and *yang* of being creative in the kitchen one night and the surprise of having dinner cooked for me the next. We share stories about everything, from what we did in school today (he's a teacher too) to personal incidents and insights, taking this time each day to relax and celebrate life together.

You can begin one mindful practice in your household by making your evening meal a celebration of life, a time to enjoy food and conversation with the ones you love. If you live alone, you can still make dinner a mindful practice. Instead of eating a frozen dinner in front of the TV or filling up on junk food, make yourself a healthy, balanced meal—don't you deserve it?—listen to your favorite music, and pause to reflect on the gift of today.

## CREATING HARMONY BETWEEN HOME AND WORK

CREATING GREATER balance between home and work will also add greater peace to your life. Many people today never leave work. They not only work longer hours, but their work follows them home in briefcases, on cell phones, voice mail, E-mail, and faxes. Electronic conveniences have become high-tech space invaders, carving up our private time, plugging us into work wherever we go. One couple I know took their laptops to check their E-mail while honeymooning in Hawaii.

The expression "Get a life" is no joke to many college students. One woman told me about her roommate, Gail, an electrical engineering major who "just works all the time." When she has a big project due, Gail sits at her computer and doesn't eat for days. Her regular routine is not much better. Snacking on junk food on her way to the computer lab, wearing the same jeans, T-shirt, and baseball cap, she comes home only to sleep and takes one shower a week—on Friday nights—as a concession to weekends.

Stressed-out college students aren't the only ones who never come home. According to research by Arlie Russell Hochschild, many women work overtime to avoid the gridlock of domestic responsibilities. Sitting at their desks to complete projects gives them an illusion of control they can't find at home with family members clamoring for their attention and the piles of dirty dishes, diapers, laundry, and other chores they face at the end of the day.[8]

Overcoming the work/home imbalance means bucking the tide of our frantic, workaholic culture. It requires a strong will and some subversive measures. But it can be done by taking small steps to get your life back in balance.

You can begin by setting limits at work. Unless there's a *real* emergency, make it a point to keep regular hours. Learn to recognize the habits that steal time from your life. If you've been staying late to finish what's on your desk, write yourself a note about where to pick up the work tomorrow— and walk out the door. I used to be so duty-bound that I'd go back to my desk after a late afternoon meeting to check my E-mail and voice mail, spending my personal, after-work hours processing trivia. I'd finally leave for home—cold, hungry, and exhausted. Getting home so late, I'd miss my workouts, postpone my errands, and have very little time to reflect, center, and enjoy my own life. Staying at work had become such a mindless habit that in order to break it I began setting an alarm at four-thirty so I could begin wrapping up in time to leave at five.

If you've been staying at work to avoid drudgery at home, you can shift the balance by making homelife more attractive. Give yourself a good reason to come home. Not more responsibilities, not more people who need you—a *good* reason, something to look forward to. A few years ago, when I took on new responsibilities at work, I got a puppy, who ended up being my best form of stress management. She'd greet me at the end of the day with her tiny face looking up eagerly, her eyes shining and tail wagging, ready to play.

I'd tell people, "I have to go home and let my dog out." Actually, having the dog let *me* out of excessive commitments. Despite the allure of all that "important" work, it was suddenly more fun at the end of the day to be at home, playing on the floor with my puppy and getting back in touch with the kid inside myself.

This year I planted a vegetable garden in the backyard. It will be great to eat home-grown produce later in the summer, but right now, my garden is a great escape. At the end of the day, I come home eager to see what's happening in the garden. Growing your own vegetables is a wonderful way to stay in touch with nature and the ongoing process of life. There's always something new in a garden. This week, new seeds have sprouted. The green beans, spinach, and carrots have come up. Flowers are blooming on the squash and tomatoes. For me, having a garden is fun, entertaining, and relaxing.

If you've been living a life out of balance, if home has become just a place to do chores, create something you'll enjoy coming home to. If your homelife has faded into gray routine, put some color back into your life. Plant geraniums on your windowsill. Get out your favorite dishes and linens and *use them*. Put new sheets on your bed or bright new towels in the bathroom. Treat yourself. Revive an old hobby you enjoyed as a girl—playing a musical instrument, weaving, doing calligraphy. Give yourself some time at the end of the day to do it—even if it's only twenty minutes. Tell your family this is your private time, be consistent, and they'll learn to respect it.

Begin reclaiming time for yourself and recognizing that there's much more to life than the work you do. Begin celebrating your life. Now.

As we create greater harmony in our lives, we move on to create greater harmony in our world. Abraham Maslow's theory of self-actualization says that when people meet their "deficiency needs"—air, water, food, shelter, and love—they naturally reach out to the world around them.[9] Our search for joy and meaning cannot occur in isolation. Whether we realize it or not, we live in ongoing relationship with the people around us and the complex cycle of life on this planet.

Living more harmoniously for Vicki Robin means eliminating frivolous purchases, "gazingus-pins," as she calls them, in order to live a simpler, freer life. Because her simpler lifestyle makes fewer demands on the planet's limited resources, it's less damaging to the environment. Vicki's plan for a simpler life is described in her book, *Your Money or Your Life*, which offers a detailed program for achieving greater personal freedom through financial independence.[10]

You can begin simplifying your own life by reducing personal and planetary waste, eliminating one mindless habit at a time. Composting and recycling are obvious ways. But what about sharing magazines with a friend, cutting down on expenses for both of you while producing less environmental waste? Spending an afternoon at the library instead of the shopping mall? Asking "Do I really need this?" before your next purchase? Creating your own holiday tradition of exchanging meals with friends instead of mindless gift-giving?

Who are we as women and what do we value? Now, more than ever, we have the opportunity, and some would say the responsibility, of reaching out with our hearts and minds to make a positive difference in our world. We all know women who are making a difference. My friend Elizabeth Moran, a retired college professor, volunteers at the Georgia Travis Center, which provides day facilities, career counseling, and personal support for homeless women and children. Recently, Elizabeth wrote a grant proposal to set up a new phone system for the center, enabling the women to get voice-mail messages, which helps when they're looking for work. In ways from the practical to the personal, Elizabeth and other volunteers reach out to these women in transition, helping them move on to better lives.

Bobbi Hall, a young mother and administrative assistant, went to Tanzania last summer on a church-sponsored project to provide English language instruction to the Zaramo people in Dar-es-Salaam. Three years ago, her congregation decided to put their faith to work and share their skills with people in another part of the world. Teaching English to people outside the United States is "a wonderful gift," says Bobbi. Learning English helps people raise themselves beyond subsistence living, getting jobs at airports and hotels.

In addition to teaching English, each team of volunteers shares their special skills. On an earlier trip, Bobbi's husband, Steve, a contractor, helped people build and repair their homes. Last year, Bobbi's musical group offered them a special gift of song along with new language skills.

This is not the first time Bobbi and Steve have shared their gifts with people around the world. In the summer of 1993, they taught English in Slovakia to people from ages eight to seventy. Their daughter, Ashley, age eleven, also benefits from the stories they bring back. She not only knows more about geography than most children her age, but also excels in her studies with the sense of agency that comes from knowing that someday she, too, can make a difference in the world.[11]

Reaching out to create greater harmony, transcending ourselves as individuals, we realize our fullest potential. Research psychologist Cecelia Hurwich found in her study of vital women in their seventies, eighties, and nineties that they were all actively working for a cause they believed in, something beyond themselves and their immediate families. Such creative work is life-affirming in the profoundest of ways, enriching our world while giving our lives greater depth and meaning.[12]

## CREATING HARMONY IN YOUR HEART

THERE ARE many stories in *The Tao of Womanhood*, woven deep and wide with all the patterns available to women today. But the final story must be your own, following your heart and finding your own path to harmony.

The path for each of us begins within. Whatever your faith, a harmonious life is a mindful life. Taking time to reflect upon the beauty around you, the gifts and lessons of each day, will help you become more centered, more focused, more aware of your own possibilities.

As much as possible, find a way to get back in touch with the wisdom of nature, whether that means taking walks in the woods or a local park, starting a garden or a few pots of herbs on a sunny windowsill. Watch the cycles of the seasons, the ongoing process of life in all its colorful dramas and quiet subtleties, realizing that you, too, are part of this pattern of growth and renewal.

Take time to listen to your own quiet thoughts. Set aside time each day to meditate or reflect on the meaning in your life. Keep a journal. Be kind to yourself, tending to your needs for healthy food, rest, and recreation. Realize, as you weave the daily pattern of your life, what strands are most important to you. Let these primary colors stand out, clear and true, against the background of demands and opportunities. Make mindful choices, setting aside some possibilities in order to follow your heart.

As the *Tao* reminds us, each day, each moment, is the beginning of a pattern much larger than itself:

*A tree that grows beyond your reach*
*Springs from a tiny seed.*
*A building more than nine stories high*
*Begins with a handful of earth.*
*A journey of a thousand miles*
*Begins with a single step.*
TAO, 64[13]

Your choices, the daily details of your life, are stepping-stones on the path to greater power and peace. Moving forward on this journey of discovery, you add your own dimension to *The Tao of Womanhood*, creating new stories of what women may be, new patterns of joy and meaning to heal and transform our world.

# Pointers for Greater Power and Peace

*Here are more ways to create greater harmony.*

■ *Practice resolving conflict by focusing on shared needs.*

Effective conflict resolution will help you reduce stress and build stronger relationships. Here are some steps to get you started:

- *Remember that conflict is natural.* Neither good nor bad, it just *is*.
- *You are not being rude when you bring up a conflict.* Identifying conflict is the first step toward resolution.
- *Get beyond anxiety and frustration* in order to focus on your needs. First release tension. Some people take a deep breath and slowly let go. Others go off by themselves for a brief "cooling off" period. By releasing your initial anger and anxiety, you can respond from a more centered space.
- *Identify what you need,* not what you want—needs are more fundamental, less specific to the situation.
- *Arrange to meet with the other person* to work on the conflict together. Find a place where you both feel comfortable and where you won't be interrupted.
- *Begin the meeting with a positive opening.* Tell the other person that you value the relationship. Refer to a positive experience in the past or a time when you worked together successfully.
- *Listen and try not to react.* Remember, this person has not learned the partnership skills, so he or she may still need to let off steam.

- *Ask the person what he or she needs.* Keep the focus on need, not what you did or should have done. Don't let the other person push your buttons. Keep asking about needs and keep listening.
- *Listen with respect* when the other person tells you what he or she needs.
- *Then tell the person what you need* as honestly and clearly as possible without falling into old habits of polarization or blame.
- *Identify the relationship needs.* As you each have your personal needs, the relationship has its needs. These are your shared needs.
- *Together, come up with some things both of you can do* to meet your needs—yours, the other person's, and the relationship's.
- *Work your plan, one step at a time.* Remember, creative conflict resolution is a process of discovery. There are no quick fixes or instant solutions. The process of working together *is* the resolution. Be patient with this process.
- *Check in with the other person to see how you're doing.* Listen and give positive reinforcement. Keep moving forward, one step at a time.[14]

Learning effective conflict resolution takes courage—*yang*—but draws upon lots of the *yin* skills familiar to women. Once you take that courageous first step, you can draw upon your *yin* skills of conversation, listening, and empathy, building bridges where there were once only barriers.

■ *Eliminate Mindless Habits/Develop Mindful Practice.*

Replacing *mindless habits* with *mindful practice* will create greater peace, power, and harmony in your life. Begin slowly, taking one area at a time, beginning where you live.

Can you identify one *mindless habit* that has been sapping your energy, stealing your time, or cluttering your life at home?

- Mindless TV watching?
- Spending too much time on the telephone?
- Mindless snacking—eating a box of crackers without thinking?
- Mindless litter—letting mail and old magazines pile up?
- Mindless dining—subsisting on a diet of frozen dinners?
- Something else?

Find a way to eliminate the mindless habit. Write yourself a reminder—in your planner, calendar, or somewhere else you'll see it each morning. Try eliminating the habit for a week and see how it feels. Next week, ask yourself how you can add one *mindful practice* to your homelife.

- Mindfully enjoying your evening meal?
- Taking a walk with your partner or child at the end of the day?
- Reading a story to your child each night?
- Reading something you enjoy or would like to know more about—a period of history, a person, a subject you're curious about? A new dimension to your life is as close as the nearest bookstore or public library.
- Taking quiet time for yourself each day to decompress and come back to center?
- Picking up a favorite hobby and setting aside time to do it regularly?
- Something else?

Try your new practice for a month and see how this works for you. Next month, work to eliminate one more mindless habit and add one more mindful practice, moving, as the spirit leads you, from home to the home/work balance, to the larger world, and back again to personal harmony in your own heart, reviewing the lessons in this chapter.

Gently making these small adjustments will help your life flow more harmoniously, according to your own natural rhythms.

# 力 Glossary

AGENCY: The ability to act or exert power over your own life. Chapter 9 shows how to develop greater agency.

AHIMSA: The principle, practiced by Buddhists and Hindus, of avoiding harm to any living being. As Chapter 3 explains, this also includes yourself.

AIKIDO: A nonviolent martial art developed in twentieth-century Japan by Morihei Ueshiba, or O Sensei. Based upon ancient samurai exercises, aikido (*ai* = harmony, *ki* = energy, *do* = the way) seeks to resolve conflict without harming the attacker.

AUTUMN: The third stage in any process, the season of harvest or completion as described in Chapter 5. In our adult life cycle, discussed in Chapter 9, autumn is middle life, which extends through our forties and fifties.

BUDO: Literally, "the way of the warrior," a martial art and inner discipline. In Chapter 4, *budo* refers to the warrior work of maintaining your own boundaries.

CATASTROPHIZING: Blowing problems out of proportion, which keeps us from solving them effectively. Chapter 10 shows how to overcome this habit.

CENTER: Being in touch with yourself at a deep level, aware of your own energies, values, and priorities. When you are *un*centered, you are reactive and easily manipulated. Chapter 2 shows how to become more centered.

CHI: The Chinese term for the energy of existence and your own vital energy. The Japanese term is *ki*. Chapter 8 tells how to renew your *chi*.

CIRCADIAN RHYTHMS: Your own daily energy cycle. Chapter 5 shows how to recognize and work with it.

COMPASSION: True compassion (described in Chapter 3) means nurturing yourself as well as others, bringing your life greater power and meaning.

COURAGE: The courage of Tao is not so much the courage to climb Mount Everest as the courage to live your own life. Chapter 7 shows how to increase your courage.

DEFINING MOMENT: A personal victory or accomplishment in adolescence when you reached out with agency and found a new sense of personal power. Chapter 9 describes how to learn from your defining moments.

DOJO: An aikido training hall.

FLOW: The *Tao* teaches that life occurs in dynamic movement—flow. Chapter 1 shows how to find greater peace of mind through flow, by seeing how the different parts of your life come together in dynamic harmony.

GI: The white jacket and pants used for training in aikido and other martial arts.

HAKAMA: The black pleated split pants, adapted from the costume of the samurai, worn by higher-ranking aikido practitioners.

HARA: The one point or center of power in aikido, located about two inches below the navel. By breathing into your *hara* you can release tension and return to center.

HEART CENTER: The character for heart (*shin* in Chinese and Japanese) means "heart-mind" or "heart-center," the center of all consciousness and motivation.

HONORABLE CLOSURE: The art of ending a project, relationship, or stage of your life with understanding and respect. Chapter 6 describes the art of honorable closure.

KARATE: A Japanese martial art that literally means "empty (*kara*) hand (*te*)." Karate practitioners use kicks and punches to defend against attacks. Advanced students can extend their *ki* to break bricks and boards with their bare hands.

KI: The Japanese term for the energy of existence and your own vital energy. The Chinese term is *chi*. Chapter 8 tells how to renew your *ki*.

KIAI: In the martial arts, a piercing shout used to focus and extend *ki*. Chapter 2 offers a *kiai* exercise to develop your ability to say no.

MA-AI: An interval, a term from aikido that means the distance in time or space between two actions, two people, two objects. In the timing of your life, *ma-ai* (described in Chapter 6) is the essential interval between action and response that enables you to live more mindfully.

**MISOGI:** Literally, in Japanese, "ritualistic cleansing." Chapter 4 shows how you can bring greater peace to your life by performing a form of *misogi* in your home.

**MUSUBI:** In the Japanese martial arts, *musubi* means the synergy of two or more energies in a single action. Chapter 6 shows how you can use *musubi* to improve the timing in your life.

**NAGE:** In aikido, the person who performs the technique, throwing the opponent.

**PERSONAL POWER:** The power that makes you who you are: your energy, values, integrity, and spiritual strength. Personal power lasts a lifetime, outlasting the power of rank or position. Chapter 8 shows how to build your personal power.

**POLARIZING:** A reductive dualism that makes people in the Western world see differences as irreconcilable opposites: either/or, all or nothing, us or them. Chapter 10 shows how to overcome polarizing.

**POSITIONAL POWER:** Power based upon externals: rank or position. Positional power is only temporary, while personal power is rooted in strength of character.

**RUBRICIZE:** To perceive someone as a function, not a person. Claiming our full potential as women means recognizing that we are always more than what we do.

**SAMURAI:** The warrior class of men and women in medieval Japan who lived by a code of honor and were known for their courage and martial prowess.

**SOCIAL ANXIETY:** Fear of embarrassment or making mistakes in public that keeps many people from learning new skills. Chapter 7 shows how to overcome this.

**SPACE INVADER:** Boundary violators, people who invade your territory when you're trying to do something else. Chapter 4 tells how to discourage space invaders.

**SPRING:** The first stage in any process, the season of initiation or new beginnings, as described in Chapter 5. In our adult life cycle, discussed in Chapter 9, spring is the season of young womanhood, from our early teens to our mid-twenties.

**SUMMER:** The second stage in any process, the season of creative growth, as described in Chapter 5. In our adult life cycle, discussed in Chapter 9, summer is the season of life that extends from our late twenties into our early forties.

**T'AI CHI CH'UAN:** Ancient Chinese practice using slow, flowing movements. Originally a martial art, it is now used primarily for relaxation and healing.

**TAO:** In Chinese means "the path" or "the way." The term can mean the teachings of Taoism. But in this book, the primary meaning is your life, an ongoing journey of discovery as you define for yourself what it means to be a woman today.

*TAO TE CHING* (abbreviated as the *Tao*): The ancient Chinese book of wisdom written twenty-five centuries ago by Lao-tzu. This short book of eighty-one poems has been translated more than any book but the Bible. Its wisdom drawn from nature is as real today as it was twenty-five centuries ago.

**TE:** The second character in the title of the *Tao Te Ching*, which has been translated variously as "strength," "character," and "power."

**TIME BANDITS:** Boundary violators, people who waste your time with trivial conversations, complaints, or problems. Chapter 4 tells how to discourage time bandits.

**TIMING:** The dynamic awareness of Tao makes you more proactive about time management. Chapter 6 shows how to avoid over-commitment, prevent procrastination, and leave a situation that no longer serves you.

**UKE:** In aikido, the attacker, the one who is thrown by the *nage* or defender.

**WINTER:** The fourth and final stage in any process, the season of contemplation, as described in Chapter 5. In our adult life cycle, discussed in Chapter 9, winter is the season of wisdom and serenity in late adulthood.

**WUSHIN:** From the Chinese *wu* ("nothingness") and *shin* ("heart-mind"), this term means a state of inner peace with no ego blocks, grudges, or prejudice. Chapter 3 ends with a daily meditation to develop *wushin*.

**YANG:** The active principle in Taoist philosophy, which sees all life as composed of *yang* and *yin*, active and contemplative, sunlight and shadow.

YIN: The contemplative principle in Taoist philosophy, which sees all life as composed of *yin* and *yang*, nurturing and assertive, night and day.

YOHAKU: Literally "white space" in Japanese, the background or margin essential to Asian art. In the art of your life, *yohaku* (described in Chapter 4) is the open space of contemplation that brings you greater peace and creative power.

# 道 Notes

INTRODUCTION

1. This passage from Chapter 62 of the *Tao Te Ching* is from my own poetic translation. All future references to the *Tao Te Ching* in this book are from my version and will be identified by chapter numbers for easy comparison with other translations.

   In this book, when *Tao* is italicized, it refers to the *Tao Te Ching*. Otherwise, the Tao means the teachings of Taoism or the life force described in the *Tao Te Ching*, the mysterious Tao that incorporates all existence. Some take the Tao to mean "the way of life" or "the path," its literal translation from the Chinese. In *The Tao of Womanhood*, it becomes a new way of seeing life, a way of living more mindfully, combining the polarities of power and peace.

   The author and publisher are grateful to HarperCollins Publishers for granting permission to include my poetic translations of *Tao* Chapters 1, 8, 16, 56, 64, 70, and 71, previously published in *The Tao of Personal Leadership* by Diane Dreher (New York: Harper-Collins Publishers, 1996).

2. As C. Margaret Hall's research has shown, women's development "includes our acceptance of our own uniqueness and the special circumstances of our lives. When we acknowledge who and where we are, we move away from conformity as an end in itself." *Women and Identity: Value Choices in a Changing World* (New York: Hemisphere, 1990), p. 79.

3. Carol Gilligan, *In a Different Voice* (Cambridge, Mass.: Harvard University Press, 1993), p. 221. See also Nancy Chodorow, "Family Structure and Feminine Personality," in M. Z. Rosaldo and Louise

Lamphere, eds. *Woman, Culture, and Society* (Stanford, Calif.: Stanford University Press, 1974), pp. 43–66.
4. Hall, op cit. pp. 32, 100.

CHAPTER 1: THE LESSON OF ONENESS

1. Libby Dale's story as told to Diane Dreher in an interview on May 1, 1997. Used with permission. For a contemporary psychologist's definition of flow, see Mihaly Csikszentmihalyi, *Finding Flow* (New York: HarperCollins, 1997).
2. Downes, Peggy, Ilene Tuttle, Patricia Faul, and Virginia Mudd, *The New Older Woman* (Berkeley, Calif.: Celestial Arts, 1996), p. 11. Reprinted by permission of Celestial Arts Publishing.
3. Abraham Maslow, "Self-Actualizing People: A Study of Psychological Health," in *Dominance, Self-Esteem, Self-Actualization: Germinal Papers of A. H. Maslow*, ed. Richard J. Lowry (Monterey, Calif.: Brooks/Cole, 1973), p. 190.


CHAPTER 2: THE LESSON OF CENTERING

1. My thanks to my colleague Claudia Mon Pere McIsaac, poet and creative writing instructor in the English department at Santa Clara University for her inspiring example and for sharing her story, used here with permission.
2. My thanks to Genevieve and Lyle Farrow for years of wisdom and friendship and for sharing the story recorded here. Used here with permission.
3. The five cards are a good beginning, but if you want to gain even greater control of the time in your life, read Hyrum Smith's book, *The 10 Natural Laws of Successful Time and Life Management* (New York: Warner Books, 1994), which discusses the A,B,C system on page 106, used here by permission of the publisher. Or get a Franklin Day Planner. For more information and a free catalog, call Franklin Quest at 1-800-654-1776 or write to P.O. Box 25127, Salt Lake City, Utah 84125-0127.
4. Henry David Thoreau, *The Variorum Walden*, ed. Walter Harding (New York: Washington Square Press, 1967), p. 68.
5. Dr. Christiane Northrup, *Creating Health*, from her *Health Wisdom for Women Reports* (Potomac, Md.: Phillips Publishing Inc., 1996),

p. 8, used here by permission. For more of Dr. Northrup's advice on women's health, see her book *Women's Bodies, Women's Wisdom* (New York: Bantam, 1994).

6. My thanks to Judy Kasper of the English department at Santa Clara University for her personal example, friendship, and support. Reference here used by permission.

## CHAPTER 3: THE LESSON OF COMPASSION

1. Poetic translation of the *Tao Te Ching*, Chapter 1, from *The Tao of Personal Leadership* by Diane Dreher (New York: HarperCollins, 1996), pp. 107–108, used here by permission of HarperCollins.

2. As humans, we *need* to care and be cared for. Many studies have revealed the healing power of compassion. Caring for a dog, cat, or even a plant has achieved remarkable results in autistic children and increased the vitality and life span of older people in long-term care facilities. See Abraham Maslow's descriptions of love and care as essential to human health in "Self-Actualizing People: A Study of Psychological Health" in *Dominance, Self-Esteem, Self-Actualization: Germinal Papers of A. H. Maslow*, ed. Richard J. Lowry (Monterey, Calif.: Brooks/Cole, 1973), pp. 197–200, and the work of Dr. Kenneth Pelletier, Senior Research Scientist and Clinical Associate Professor of Medicine at the Stanford Medical School, who spoke about the healing power of compassion on KQED Radio's *Forum* in an interview in San Francisco with Michael Krasny on May 8, 1997. His latest book is *Sound Mind, Sound Body* (New York: Simon & Schuster, 1994).

3. Anna Eleanor Roosevelt from *This Is My Story* (1937), quoted in *Bartlett's Familiar Quotations*, 16th edition, ed. John Bartlett, rev. and enl., ed. Justin Kaplan (New York: Little Brown and Co., 1992), p. 654.

4. Carol Gilligan, Letter to Readers in *In a Different Voice: Psychological Theory and Women's Development* (Cambridge, Mass.: Harvard University Press, 1993), p. xiii. Used here by permission.

5. My thanks to Sunny Skys and Miki Yoneda-Skys, for lessons in aikido and life, as well as for the beautiful calligraphy in this book. They can be reached at Aiki Zenshin Dojo/Aikido of Fremont, 42307 Osgood Road, Unit J, Fremont, Calif. 94539; 510-657-5387. Their story used by permission.

6. Psychologists interviewed in 1995 said that the majority of women have "a body image disorder." From "Making Friends with Your Body" by Dianne Hales and Christina Frank, *Fitness*, June 1995, p. 102.

7. "The Athletic Esthetic" by Holly Brubach, *The New York Times Magazine*, June 23, 1996, Section 6, pp. 48–51.

8. My thanks to Marlene Bjornsrud, currently assistant athletic director at Santa Clara University, for her insights during a conversation on May 9, 1997, used here by permission.

### CHAPTER 4: THE LESSON OF SIMPLICITY

1. Henry David Thoreau, *The Variorum Walden*, ed. Walter Harding (New York: Washington Square Press, 1962), p. 83.

2. Frank Goble, *The Third Force: The Psychology of Abraham Maslow* (New York: Pocket Books, 1971), p. 44.

3. Jean Baker Miller, *Toward a New Psychology of Women* (Boston: Beacon Press, 1986), p. 110.

### CHAPTER 5: THE LESSON OF NATURAL CYCLES

1. My poetic translation of the *Tao Te Ching*, Chapter 16 from *The Tao of Personal Leadership* by Diane Dreher (New York: Harper-Collins, 1996), p. 236. Used with permission of HarperCollins.

2. In *Women's Bodies, Women's Wisdom* (New York: Bantam, 1995), holistic gynecologist Dr. Christiane Northrup says, "Studies have shown that peak conception rates and probably ovulation appear to occur at the full moon or the day before. During the new moon, ovulation and conception rates are decreased overall, and an increased number of women start their menstrual bleeding. Scientific research has determined that the moon rules the flow of fluids (ocean tides as well as individual body fluids) and affects the unconscious and dreams" (p. 97). Used with permission.

3. Dr. Christiane Northrup, *Health Wisdom for Women*, Vol. 2., No.8 (August 1996), pp. 1–3, used with permission. For further information or to subscribe to this publication, call 1-800-211-8561 or write Phillips Publishing Inc., P.O. Box 60042, 7811 Montrose Road, Potomac, Md. 20859-0042. Dr. Northrup's book, *Women's Bodies, Women's Wisdom*, cited above, explains how women can

bring greater harmony to their lives by developing greater understanding and acceptance of these bodily processes (pp. 95-148).

4. There are a number of sequential patterns proposed as paradigms of human development. See, for example, Erik Erikson, *Childhood and Society*, 2d. ed. (1950; reprint, New York: W. W. Norton, 1963) and *Adulthood* (New York: W. W. Norton, 1978); Daniel J. Levinson, *The Seasons of a Man's Life* (New York: Alfred A. Knopf, 1978); Daniel J. and Judy D. Levinson, *The Seasons of a Woman's Life* (New York: Alfred A. Knopf, 1996); Carol Gilligan, *In a Different Voice: Psychological Theory and Women's Development* (Cambridge, Mass.: Harvard University Press, 1993); as well as Gail Sheehy's more popular *Passages* (New York: E. P. Dutton, 1976), *The Silent Passage* (New York: Simon & Schuster, 1993), and *New Passages* (New York: Random House, 1995).

5. My thanks to my brother-in-law and sister-in-law, Michael and Marilyn Numan, for their beautiful example, used here with permission.

6. For a more poetic description of the name of the house and more of Frances's story, read her beautiful memoir, *Under the Tuscan Sun: At Home in Italy* by Frances Mayes (San Francisco: Chronicle Books, 1996; and New York: Broadway Books, 1997). Her story used here with permission from Frances Mayes and Chronicle Books.

7. From an interview on National Public Radio's *Forum* with Michael Krasny, November 19, 1996.

CHAPTER 6: THE LESSON OF TIMING

1. My poetic translation of the *Tao Te Ching*, Chapter 8, from *The Tao of Personal Leadership* by Diane Dreher (New York: HarperCollins, 1996), p. 45, used here by permission of HarperCollins.

2. For a more detailed discussion of *ma-ai*, see Mitsugi Saotome, *Aikido and the Harmony of Nature* (Boston: Shambhala, 1993), pp. 167–169.

3. Ibid., p. 154. Used by permission.

4. B. Eugene Griessman, *Time Tactics of Very Successful People* (New York: McGraw-Hill, 1994), p. 76. This quote from Griessman and those that follow are used by permission of McGraw-Hill.

5. For insights about honorable closure, I am grateful to Rev. Tina Clare of Los Altos, California, for years of conversation and inspiration.
6. Griessman, op. cit., p. 98.
7. Ibid., p. 93.

CHAPTER 7: THE LESSON OF COURAGE

1. My poetic translation of the *Tao Te Ching*, Chapter 56, from *The Tao of Personal Leadership* by Diane Dreher (New York: Harper-Collins, 1996), p. 107, used here by permission of HarperCollins.
2. For research on how preadolescent girls are inhibited by our society, see Mary Pipher, *Reviving Ophelia: Saving the Selves of Adolescent Girls* (New York: Grosset/Putnam, 1994), and Emily Hancock, *The Girl Within* (New York: Dutton, 1989).
3. See Matina Horner's classic study, "Toward an Understanding of Achievement-Related Conflicts in Women," *Journal of Social Issues* 28 (1972):157–175; Carol Gilligan, *In a Different Voice: Psychological Theory and Women's Development* (Cambridge, Mass: Harvard University Press, 1993), p. ix; C. Margaret Hall, *Women and Identity: Value Choices in a Changing World* (New York: Hemisphere, 1990), p. 89.
4. Abraham Maslow, "Resistance to Being Rubricized," in *Perspectives in Psychological Theory*, ed. Bernard Kaplan and Seymour Wapner (New York: International University Press, 1960), pp. 174–175; Jean Baker Miller, *Toward a New Psychology of Women*, 2nd ed. (Boston: Beacon Press, 1986), p. 59, used here with permission.
5. Miller, p. 66, used with permission.
6. Abraham Maslow, quoted in Edward Hoffman, *The Right to be Human: A Biography of Abraham Maslow* (Los Angeles: Jeremy Tarcher, 1988), p. 298.
7. Research of S. Korchin and G. Ruff, "Personality Characteristics of the Mercury Astronauts," in G. Grosser, H. Wechsler, M. Greenblatt, eds. *The Threat of Impending Disaster* (Cambridge, Mass.: M.I.T. Press, 1964), quoted in Stanley J. Rachman, *Fear and Courage* (San Francisco: W. H.Freeman, 1978), pp. 238–239.
8. See Rachman, p. 248, for an explanation of how desensitizing works.
9. I am grateful to Tracey Kahan, Ph.D., associate professor of psy-

chology at Santa Clara University and still an expert skiier, for her insights about defining and facing our fears and the advice that follows, from an interview in Santa Clara, California, on February 12, 1997. Used with permission.

10. See "Hero" in *The Compact Edition of the Oxford English Dictionary* (New York: Oxford University. Press, 1971), p. 245.

11. Aung San Suu Kyi, quoted in "The Passion of Suu Kyi," by Claudia Dreifus, *New York Times Magazine*, Sunday, January 7, 1996, p. 36. Used with permission.

CHAPTER 8: THE LESSON OF STRENGTH

1. My thanks to Sue Ann McKean for sharing her insights on women and power in an interview at Aiki Zenshin Dojo in Fremont, California, on November 8, 1996, and in these pages. Quotes and information used here by permission.

2. Jean Baker Miller, *Toward a New Psychology of Women*, 2nd ed. (Boston: Beacon Press, 1986), p. 88, used by permission; see also Carol Gilligan, *In a Different Voice: Psychological Theory and Women's Development* (Cambridge, Mass.: Harvard University Press, 1982), p. 71.

3. For a historical discussion of this repressive feminine ideal, see Suzanne W. Hull, *Chaste, Silent, and Obedient: English Books for Women, 1475–1640* (San Marino, Calif.: The Huntington Library, 1982).

4. My thanks to Lyn and Rick Herrick for their creative example, used here with permission. Their latest books are *The Woman's Hands-on Home Repair Guide* by Lyn Herrick (Pownal, Vt.: Storey Communications, 1997) and Rick Herrick's novel, *Appalachian Love Story* (Edmonton, Alberta: Commonwealth Publications, 1997).

5. For a description of the psychological characteristics of subordinates, see Miller, op. cit., p. 7.

6. See P. Ekman, R. W. Levenson, and W. V. Friesen, "Autonomic Nervous System Activity Distinguishes Among Emotions," *Science* 223 (September 16, 1983), 1208–1210; and C. E. Izard, "Facial Expression and the Regulation of Emotions," *Journal of Personality and Social Psychology* 58 (1990): 487–498.

7. My poetic translation of the *Tao Te Ching*, Chapter 71, from *The*

*Tao of Personal Leadership* by Diane Dreher (New York: HarperCollins, 1996), p. 163, used here by permission of HarperCollins.

8. For a more complete discussion of her journey of discovery, see Frances Moore Lappé, *Diet for a Small Planet*, 10th anniversary edition (New York: Ballantine, 1982), pp. 7–57. Information here used by permission.

9. For a fuller discussion of this, see George Leonard, *Mastery* (New York: Dutton, 1991), pp. 14–15. Reference used with permission.

10. My thanks to Dr. Jane Leftwich Curry, associate professor of political science at Santa Clara University, for her friendship and inspiration. Reference used with permission.

11. See, for example, Elizabeth Davis, *Women's Intuition* (Berkeley, Calif.: Celestial Arts, 1989).


CHAPTER 9: THE LESSON OF AGENCY

1. My poetic translation of the *Tao Te Ching*, Chapter 70, from *The Tao of Personal Leadership* by Diane Dreher (New York: Harper-Collins, 1996), p. 96, used by permission of HarperCollins.

2. I am grateful to my mother, Mary Ann Hearte Dreher, from the WASP class of 1944-7 for many things, including her personal example and affirmation of what women can do.

3. Betty Friedan, *The Feminine Mystique* (New York: Norton, 1983), p. 14, used with permission.

4. Emily Hancock, *The Girl Within* (New York: Dutton, 1989), pp. 3–4, used with permission.

5. For a thorough discussion of the theories of learned helplessness and learned optimism, based on years of research, see Martin Seligman, *Learned Optimism* (New York: Alfred A. Knopf, 1991). He defines "explanatory style" on pp. 15–16. This and all other references to Seligman used with permission.

6. Ibid., p. 44. Seligman's research has revealed that these three categories make the difference between life patterns of chronic failure and long-term success.

7. Ibid., p. 15.

8. Ibid., pp. 15–16.

9. See ibid., pp. 172–281, and "Ideas and Trends: It's Called Poor Health for a Reason" by Richard A. Shweder, *The New York*

*Times,* Sunday, March 9, 1997, Section 4, "Week in Review," p. 5.

10. S. R. Maddi and S. C. Kobasa, *The Hardy Executive: Health Under Stress* (Chicago: Dorsey/Dow Jones-Irwin, 1984), pp. 31–32.

11. Mary Pipher, *Reviving Ophelia: Saving the Selves of Adolescent Girls* (New York: Ballantine, 1994), p. 23. Used with permission.

12. Ibid., pp. 49–51.

13. My thanks to Eileen Vierra for an interview in Santa Clara, California, on April 4, 1997. Reference used here with permission.

14. My thanks to my friend and colleague Sherry Booth for her comments in a conversation on March 11, 1997, used here with permission, and to all the multifaceted, creative women in my department for inspiring me with their own personal artistry.

15. Abraham Maslow, *Toward a Psychology of Being* (New York: Van Nostrand, 1962), p. 128, used with permission.

16. Carolyn G. Heilbrun, *Reinventing Womanhood* (New York: Norton, 1979), p. 15, used with permission.

17. Gail Sheehy, *The Silent Passage* (New York: Simon & Schuster, 1993), p. 121.

18. Gail Sheehy, quoted in *The New Older Woman* by Peggy Downes, Ilene Tuttle, Patricia Faul, and Virginia Mudd (Berkeley, Calif.: Celestial Arts, 1996), p. 9 (hereafter cited as Downes et al.), reprinted by permission of Celestial Arts Publishing, Berkeley, Calif.; and in Gail Sheehy, *New Passages: Mapping Your Life Across Time* (New York: Random House, 1995), p. 6 and *passim.*

19. Peggy and Chuck Downes, *Dialogue of Hope: Talking Our Way Through Cancer* (Sunflower, 1992).

20. My thanks to Dr. Peggy Downes, who teaches political science at Santa Clara University and affirms new possibilities for women in her life and work. Her story used with permission.

21. Erik Erikson describes the season of integrity in *Childhood and Society,* 2d. ed. (1995; reprint, New York: W. W. Norton, 1963), pp. 247–267. Mary Catherine Bateson is quoted in Downes et al., p. 150. Reprinted by permission of Celestial Arts Publishing, Berkeley, Calif.

22. My thanks to Genevieve Farrow and Elizabeth Moran for their many examples of agency. Their stories used with permission.

23. My thanks to Gertrude Welch for a beautiful example of living in peace. Her story used with permission.

24. Dr. Eleanor Zuckerman, in Downes et al., p. 47. Reprinted by permission of Celestial Arts Publishing, Berkeley, Calif.
25. Again, for a more thorough discussion of learned optimism and how to achieve it, see Seligman's excellent book, *Learned Optimism*, pp. 15–16 and passim. References used here with permission.

### CHAPTER 10: THE LESSON OF HARMONY

1. Abraham Maslow, *Toward a Psychology of Being* (New York: Van Nostrand, 1962), p. 38. Used with permission.
2. Jean Baker Miller, *Toward a New Psychology of Women,*. 2nd ed. (Boston: Beacon Press, 1986), p. 125. See also p. 131. Used with permission.
3. Emily Hancock, *The Girl Within* (New York: Dutton, 1989), p. 188. Used with permission.
4. My thanks to Kristie Stovall of Aiki Zenshin Dojo in Fremont for her friendship and example. Her story used with permission.
5. Dudley Weeks, *The Eight Essential Steps to Conflict Resolution* (Los Angeles: Jeremy P. Tarcher, 1992), pp. 70–87, 143. The "conflict partnership process," "shared needs," and the process of identifying and working with the three levels of needs, yours, mine, and ours, are all defined and explained much more extensively in Dudley's book and used here with permission. I am grateful to Dudley for his process, which I draw upon more every day and to Courtney Klug, Katie O'Brien, and Jeanie Kim for founding the Conflict Resolution Program at Santa Clara University.
6. Judy B. Rosener, *America's Competitive Secret: Utilizing Women as a Management Strategy* (New York: Oxford University Press, 1995), pp. 11–12, 73. Used with permission.
7. My thanks to Annette Robinson, claim education manager at Allstate Insurance, and Jill Goodman Gould, senior lecturer in English at Santa Clara University, for sharing their strategies. Their stories used with permission.
8. See *The Time Bind* by Arlie Russell Hochschild (New York: Metropolitan Books, Henry Holt & Co., 1997). Reference used with permission.
9. Abraham Maslow, "Self-Actualizing People: A Study of Psychological Health," in *Dominance, Self-Esteem, Self-Actualization: Ger-*

*minal Papers of A. H. Maslow.* ed. Richard J. Lowry (Monterey, Calif: Brooks/Cole, 1973), pp. 177–201.

10. For a revolutionary approach to personal finance, freedom, and focus, see *Your Money or Your Life: Transforming Your Relationship with Money and Achieving Financial Independence* by Joe Dominguez and Vicki Robin (New York: Penguin Books, 1993). Gazinguspins, their word for things that we don't need but can't resist buying, are defined and discussed on p. 27 and used here with permission.

11. My thanks to Elizabeth J. Moran and Bobbi Lynn Hall, for sharing their stories with me. Used here with permission.

12. Peggy Downes et al., *The New Older Woman* (Berkeley, Calif.: Celestial Arts, 1996), p. 10.

13. Poetic translation of the *Tao Te Ching*, Chapter 64, from *The Tao of Personal Leadership* by Diane Dreher (New York: HarperCollins, 1996), p. 26. Used here with permission of the publisher.

14. These steps were adapted from Weeks, op. cit., pp. 70–87. Used with permission.

# Permissions

The author and publisher gratefully acknowledge permission to use selections and information from the following copyrighted materials:

Author photograph of Diane Dreher used by permission of the photographer, Mardeene B. Mitchell.

Joe Dominguez and Vicki Robin, summary of ideas from *Your Money or Your Life* (New York: Penguin, 1992), p. 27. Included by permission of Penguin USA.

Peggy Downes, Patricia Faul, Virginia Mudd, and Ilene Tuttle, *The New Older Woman* (Berkeley, Calif.: Celestial Arts, 1996), pp. 9, 11, 47, and 150. Reprinted by permission of Celestial Arts Publishing, Berkeley, California.

Diane Dreher, quotes from poetic translations of Chapters 1, 8, 16, 56, 64, 70, and 71 of the *Tao Te Ching*, from pp. 107–08, 45, 236, 107, 164, 96, and 26 of *The Tao of Personal Leadership* by Diane Dreher (New York: HarperCollins, 1996). Copyright © 1996 by Diane Dreher. Reprinted by permission of Harper-Collins Publishers.

Claudia Dreifus, quote in "The Passion of Suu Kyi," *The New York Times Magazine*, January 7, 1996, p. 36. From *Interview*. Copyright © 1997 by Claudia Dreifus (New York: Seven Stories Press). Reprinted by permission of the publisher.

Betty Friedan, quote on p. 14 from *The Feminine Mystique* by Betty

Friedan. Copyright © 1983, 1974, 1973, 1963 by Betty Friedan. Reprinted by permission of W. W. Norton, Inc.

Carol Gilligan, quote from p. xiii of *In a Different Voice* by Carol Gilligan. Copyright © 1982, 1993 by Carol Gilligan. Reprinted by permission of Harvard University Press.

Eugene Griessman, *Time Tactics of Very Successful People* (New York: McGraw-Hill, 1994), Quotes on pp. 76, 93, and 98. Copyright © 1994 by McGraw-Hill, Inc. Reproduced by permission of the McGraw-Hill Companies.

Emily Hancock, *The Girl Within* (New York: Dutton, 1989), pp. 3–4, 188. Reproduced by permission of Penguin USA.

Carolyn Heilbrun, quote on p. 15 of *Reinventing Womanhood* (New York: Norton, 1979). Copyright © by Carolyn G. Heilbrun. Reprinted by permission of W. W. Norton & Company, Inc.

Reference to ideas from *The Time Bind* (New York: Henry Holt, 1997) by Arlie Russell Hochschild. Copyright © 1997 by Arlie Russell Hochschild. Reprinted by permission of Henry Holt and Company Inc.

Frances Moore Lappé, information adapted from *Diet for a Small Planet* (New York: Ballantine, 1982), pp. 7–75. Included by permission of Frances Moore Lappé.

George Leonard, summary of ideas from *Mastery* (New York: Dutton, 1991), pp. 14–15. Included by permission of Penguin USA.

Abraham Maslow, quotes from *Toward a Psychology of Being* (New York: Van Nostrand, 1962), pp. 38 and 128. Reprinted by permission of Van Nostrand Reinhold.

Frances Mayes, summary of material from *Under the Tuscan Sun* (San Francisco: Chronicle Books, 1996). Used by permission of Frances Mayes and Chronicle Books.

Jean Baker Miller, *Toward a New Psychology of Women* (Boston: Beacon Press, 1986), quotes from pp. 59, 66, 88, and 125. Reproduced by permission of Beacon Press.

Christiane Northrup, M.D., quote from *Women's Bodies, Women's Wisdom* (New York, Bantam, 1995), p. 97. Reprinted by permission of Bantam, Doubleday, Dell Publishing Group.